THE WHITE ROSE WAY

A 100 MILE WALKING TRAIL
FROM LEEDS TO SCARBOROUGH

BY PAUL BROWN

COPYRIGHT HAZELBURY PUBLISHING

All rights reserved. No part of this publication may be reproduced, stored in a retrieval system, transmitted in any form, by any means electrical or mechanical, or photocopied, or recorded by any other information storage and retrieval systems without prior permission in writing from the author.

Published by Hazelbury Publishing

Printed by The Amadeus Press
Fine Book and Colour Printers
Cleckheaton, BD19 4TQ

ISBN 978-0-9571134-0-4

Contents

	Page
Foreword	4
White Rose Way – The Walk	5
Mileage Chart	7
Trail Notes	8
Disclaimer	80
Photographs	81

Foreword

A sports car, driven by a young man, pulled in at the side of the road in Leeds City Square and the driver beckoned to an old man wearing a cloth cap, who was walking by.
"If you were me, which way would you get to Scarborough from here?" asked the young man.
The old man lifted his cap and scratched his head, pondering for a moment.
"If I were thee lad, I wouldn't start from here." he said, and walked on.

He may as well have asked the Black Prince.

West Yorkshire folk, or 'Wessies', as we are referred to by our East Yorkshire cousins, have made this very journey for many years, attracted from the industrial centres of West Yorkshire by the charms of what is officially Britain's first seaside resort - Scarborough.

The U.S.A. may have it's Route 66, but we have our Route A64.
Okay, it may not have the same cachet, but this road holds memories for generations of Yorkshire people as they made their way, lemming-like, to the sea.

Not all memories are happy ones, however, and there must be thousands who have cursed lengthy traffic jams at traditional bottle-necks like Tadcaster and Malton (both by-passed in the late 1970s) and the still notorious Hopgrove roundabout at York.

Often the cry went up "It'd be quicker to walk!"

Having been a keen fell and mountain walker for most of my life, I began to look into the prospect and discovered that a definitive walk from Leeds to Scarborough didn't exist.

Until now.

I would like to thank my long suffering wife Sally, who has supported me throughout this project, providing tea, packed lunches, transport and encouragement in equal measure.

Grateful thanks to David and John at Amadeus and to John at the Long Distance Walker's Association for help and advice.

Thanks also, to Mick, Ken, Eileen, Barry, Jeff, Chris, Gareth and Vikki, for their company and assistance in walking all of the sections, some many times over, to get things just right. Respect too, to Gareth, Sarah and Ben for help and advice with drawings, the web-site, design and computer related thing-gummies which are sometimes beyond an oldie like me.

May I also give a nod, to all the historians, archivists, web-site compilers and helpful library staff too numerous to mention, for providing the basic information from which the many points of interest have been researched and composed.
This is not just a guided walk - it is a walk through time.

Finally, I wish all those undertaking this route all the best for an enjoyable and rewarding experience.

White Rose Way – The Walk

This route, like the sports car driver, begins a journey to Scarborough from the Black Prince statue in Leeds' City Square.

Ultra modern and Victorian developments give way to ribbons of parkland, following sections of The Dales Way link and the Ebor Way to Wetherby.

Continuing across vast agricultural plains, the walk passes through Boston Spa and Tadcaster, before following an old Roman road into suburbs of the city of York.

From here, we link up with the Minster Way, on to historic Stamford Bridge and the River Derwent. We then head upriver through the Howardian Hills Area of Outstanding Natural Beauty to join the Centenary Way into Malton and the chocolate-box village of Thornton Le Dale.

Forestry now dominates as the path pushes deep into the North York Moors National Park and the impossibly beautiful Dalby Forest, along part of The Blue Man Walk, into Wykeham Forest and then alongside the infant Derwent into remote Harwood Dale.

The final stretch fills the nostrils with sea air as we hit the coast and drop southwards on the cliff tops, along the Cleveland Way.

A beach and headland walk around the magnificent Scarborough Castle completes the journey as we reach the glorious South Bay, and the finish line.

This is a truly varied and magnificent, one hundred mile walk (ok 104.4, who's counting?).
It may be slightly slower than the A64, but it is ultimately much more rewarding.

The walk itself, although lengthy, is comparable in many ways to a number of National Trails and links sections of several established walks.

There are no mountains to conquer, nor even any significant hills. It can be completed fairly easily by reasonably fit walkers.

For the majority of the route, we are talking flat, open countryside, easy going underfoot and well defined footpaths.
The walk is non-prescriptive, allowing walkers to choose the length of the days walk and accommodation where you wish to stop for the night. Fitter walkers and runners may complete the walk in three or four days, whilst some may take a week. Others may wish to complete it at leisure, over a series of single days or week-ends. The choice is yours.

As an example of the flexibility, there is the option to stay overnight at Harewood after ten miles on the first day, for those who desire a gentler introduction, or to push on to Linton, Wetherby and beyond.
The penultimate leg traverses Dalby and Wykeham Forests and heads into remote areas before emerging into Harwood Dale.

The route may be completed at any time of year. It should be borne in mind however, that in smaller villages, and Harwood Dale in particular, accommodation may be limited or subject to seasonal opening from March to November.

I would strongly advise that if you intend to stay overnight in Harwood Dale, book in advance, start your series of bookings here and work backwards from there.
The alternative solution is to extend this leg and push on towards the Cloughton area.

This route can be undertaken simply by following the detailed walk instructions and indeed it has been done this way without difficulty by a number of my friends, or guinea pigs, as I prefer to call them.

I would always advise walkers to carry relevant maps (O.S. 1:25,000 Explorer) and a compass, and have the necessary knowledge of how to use them. An emergency may arise unexpectedly and you will need to know exactly where you are.

A list of suggested accommodation can be found at www.whiteroseway.co.uk

First aid kits and associated equipment should always be carried.
Always follow the Countryside Code – leave only footprints, take only memories.

Points of Interest

Throughout this walk, I have researched and inserted snippets of information about features and places through which the route passes.
It contains historical information about people and places, facts and figures and the occasional oddity.

Why, for example, did the Black Prince never become King?

Where can you find a 200 year old pear tree?

What did the Romans ever do for us?

How did 28,000 men come to be killed on a single site?

Where does the bloodline of 85% of English racehorses come from?

Who was the 'Railway King'?

Why is this house the most photographed in Britain?

How did a Bronte sister come to be buried here and not Haworth?

Where is the longest railway station seat in the world?

These are just a taste of the many gems you will find.

I hope they add to your enjoyment.

White Rose Way

From	To	Miles	Km	Walking Time	Page
CITY SQUARE	HAREWOOD	10.8	17.4	4h.15m	8
HAREWOOD	LINTON	7.0	11.3	2h.20m	21
LINTON	WETHERBY	1.8	2.9	0h.40m	25
WETHERBY	BOSTON SPA	3.1	5.0	1h.30m	28
BOSTON SPA	TADCASTER	5.3	8.4	2h.00m	31
TADCASTER	BISHOPTHORPE	7.7	12.4	2h.45m	36
BISHOPTHORPE	FULFORD	3.1	5.1	1h.15m	41
FULFORD	KEXBY	9.2	14.8	3h 00m	45
KEXBY	STAMFORD BRIDGE	3.2	5.4	1h 20m	49
STAMFORD BRIDGE	MALTON	16.3	25.9	6h 00m	53
MALTON	THORNTON LE DALE	10.2	16.4	3h50m	61
THORNTON LE DALE	HARWOOD DALE	15.7	25.4	5h 45m	65
HARWOOD DALE	CLOUGHTON	4.2	6.7	1h 50m	72
CLOUGHTON	SCARBOROUGH	6.8	10.9	2h 20m	76
	TOTAL	104.4	168.0		

The walking time is shown for guidance only and is at a reasonable pace, taking no account of breaks, mealtimes, chatting to local people or simply enjoying the view. Allow extra time for these essentials!

White Rose Way – Leeds to Scarborough

Walk instructions are shown in normal type.
Points of interest are shown as you reach them and are in **bold** type.
All distances shown in metres are approximate – the section mileage totals are exact.
Read what it says – not what you think it says!

City Square to Harewood (10 .8 miles, 17.4 km)

The walk begins at the base of the Black Prince statue in Leeds City Square.

City Square was completed in 1899, at the behest of Leeds City Council.
Plans did exist for an underground railway system based under the square, but regretfully, these plans never came to fruition. What a boon this would have been for modern Leeds.
The square has seen several transformations over the years and was configured to its present arrangement in the early 2000's.
It contains the statues of local luminaries, but the most striking is that of the 'Black Prince,' on horseback.
It features Edward of Woodstock (1330-1376), son of King Edward III and father of King Richard II.
He was appointed as the Prince of Wales in 1343, at the age of 13.
As an adult, he became noted for victories in battles against the French, most significantly at Crecy and Poitiers.
Edward died a year before his father and so never became King.
He was not known as the Black Prince until some 200 years after his death and he has no known connections with Leeds.
The statue was commissioned as a symbol of the virtues of chivalry and democracy by the donor, Colonel Thomas Harding, a former Lord Mayor of Leeds.

Stand with your back to the Queens Hotel and start out half-right, leaving City Square by means of the pedestrian controlled traffic light crossing, into Park Row, and walk on the left side pavement.

Pass the first pedestrianised street on your left, at traffic lights, and continue, to pass four side streets on your left, reaching the major crossroads junction of Park Row with The Headrow.
Leeds Town Hall is away to your left.

Leeds Town Hall was completed in 1858, and was designed by Cuthbert Broderick, the famous Hull born Victorian architect.
It was opened by Queen Victoria and Prince Albert in September of that year.
The building contained Crown and Magistrates Courts, together with police holding cells or 'Bridewell' and these were in use until 1993, when a new Combined Courts Complex was opened a little further down the Headrow.
Two pairs of Portland stone lions were added to the frontage on 1867.

Folklore has it that they roam the streets at night, rounding up lost children.
The notorious house-breaker and police murderer Charlie Peace (1832 – 1879) was held in the Bridewell cells prior to his trial and subsequent hanging in 1879.
He is one of very few real criminals ever mentioned in the books of Sir Arthur Conan Doyle. Sherlock Holmes referred to him in the short story 'The Adventure of the Illustrious Client,' written in 1924.
The main hall contains one of the largest concert organs in Europe.
Today, the Town Hall is used for music concerts and civic functions.
It is also the home of the triennial and world renowned, Leeds International Pianoforte Competition.

Using the traffic light controlled crossing, carry on straight across the Headrow, into Cookridge Street.

The Henry Moore Institute, on your immediate left, is the home to many pieces created by world famous sculptor, Henry Moore (1898 – 1986).
Moore was born in nearby Castleford and he is most well known for large abstract bronze works, mainly depicting the human form.
One can be seen on a plinth to the left, outside the Institute.
The building itself, was created from Victorian merchant's offices, which were refurbished and extended.

Still on the left pavement, continue along Cookridge Street.

St. Anne's Cathedral, was first built in 1838, and originally stood at the corner of The Headrow and Cookridge Street.
Redevelopment plans led to its demolition and the new Cathedral was built on its present site, on your right.
This was opened in 1904, and has an Arts and Crafts neo-Gothic style of architecture.

Cross straight over the junction of Cookridge Street with Great George Street.
As you come to a paved pedestrian area, carry straight on through the first set of bollards, past Leeds City Museum, which is on your right.

Pass Millennium Square and the Civic Hall, on your left.

Millennium Square, to your left, was created as part of national celebrations to mark the year 2000, built at a cost of £12,000,000.
It is a public open space and is host to various events such as concerts, German-style Christmas markets and a portable ice-rink.
It has underground changing rooms and facilities for artistes.

Leeds Civic Hall is situated at the top side of Millennium Square and is the administrative headquarters of Leeds City Council.
It was opened by King George V in 1933, and was built at a cost of £360,000.
The golden owls seen on the top of the building are the symbols of Leeds.

Follow this continuation of Cookridge Street through a second set of bollards, as the road then bears right uphill and past Leeds City College, which is on your right.

At the T- junction with the A660, Woodhouse Lane, there is a set of traffic lights.

The Merrion Centre, seen down to your right, was modelled on American shopping malls and was opened in 1964. It is typical of 1960s, 'brutalist' architecture. It was originally one of the largest of its type in Europe and was extended in 1971. The latest part conversion took place in 2005, with the opening of it's former ballroom as the Oceana nightclub.

At these lights, turn left along the footpath, to the left of metal railings.
At the end of this short path, bear right across the road to another footpath.
Continue on this path, alongside a car park on your left. (May be built on soon).
Cross the road at the pedestrian controlled traffic lights, and go straight on,
making for the white tower with a clock, which is ahead of you.

Keeping to the left hand side footpath, cross over the top of the A.58 (M), Inner Ring Road and continue straight ahead.

Old Broadcasting House, to your right, was the former home of the BBC offices and regional programming for Yorkshire.
The building is now used by Leeds Metropolitan University as a digital training facility and co-working space for start-up and freelance businesses.
The rusty looking structure and tower is the LMU Faculty of Arts, Environment and Technology. There is also accommodation for students (pictured).
It is clad in Corten weathering steel, to give it a unique appearance.
The building received two awards in 2010, as the best new tall building in Europe and best new tall building in the World, beating off rivals such as the Barj Khalifa in Dubai, and the Pinnacle in London.

The broadcasting studios which once stood to the left of the older building were demolished in 2004 when the BBC relocated to new premises in the city centre.
This was the site of workshops used by Louis Le Prince, and a blue plaque is in place here.
Louis Le Prince (1842 – 1890), was a Frenchman who worked both in England and the U.S.A.
He moved to Leeds in 1866 and it was in these workshops that he invented the first single lens camera and a projector.
He filmed 'Roundhay Garden Scene' and a second film of trams and pedestrians at Leeds Bridge, in 1888. These films were the world's first moving pictures.
They were exhibited to the public in Leeds, in what was the world's first moving picture show.
This was seven years before the work of the Lumiere Brothers and Thomas Edison, all of whom received greater public recognition in this field.
Le Prince mysteriously vanished from the Dijon to Paris train on 16th September 1890 and he was never seen again, nor was his body ever recovered.
Numerous conspiracy theories surround his disappearance.

Pass the white stone Parkinson Building with its prominent clock tower, which is part of Leeds University complex, on your left.

Leeds University can be traced to its origins in 1831, as the Leeds School of Medicine.
It has expanded significantly, to cater for around 33,000 students today.
It is currently ranked as one of the top universities in the world.
The iconic white Portland stone Parkinson Building was started in 1938, but not completed until 1951, due to World War II.

Pass Eldon Terrace and the Eldon Pub on the opposite side of the road.
Continue to the junction with Clarendon Road, at a set of traffic lights.
Cross straight over Clarendon Road, to reach pedestrian controlled traffic lights ten metres ahead of you, outside The Library Pub.

Turn right and cross the dual carriageway of Woodhouse Lane, with Woodhouse Moor, an open stretch of parkland, to your left.

Woodhouse Moor was once a much larger area and included land now occupied by Leeds University buildings.
It has long been a military gathering point, notably in January 1643, when Sir William Savile defended Leeds against the forces of Sir Thomas Fairfax.
The Royalists were defeated, but re-took the city in June of that year.
Rampart Road is named after the fortified ramparts, which are still visible.
Bought by Leeds City Council in 1857, it was visited by Queen Victoria as part of the celebrations for the opening of Leeds Town Hall.
It is now a public park and occasional fair ground site.

Turn immediately quarter left, and walk down Raglan Road (no road sign), on the right side pavement, in front of the 'take-away' shops and restaurants.
Woodhouse Moor is still on your left.

The statue of Henry Rowland Marsden (1823 – 1876), to your left, was erected two years after his death, paid for from funds raised by 'upwards of 30,000 subscribers'.
Henry was born in Leeds to a poor background, but after emigrating to the U.S.A., he went on to make his fortune there as a mechanical engineer.
Marsden returned to Leeds, and patented a stone crushing machine, amongst other inventions, and he later became a Magistrate and Lord Mayor.
He was a philanthropist, who gave much of his fortune to good causes.
This statue also marks the starting point of the Dales Way Link and the Meanwood Valley Trail.

The Meanwood Valley Trail is a 7 mile (11km) recreational route from Woodhouse Moor to Golden Acre Park, passing along Meanwood Ridge, through Meanwood Park and Scotland Wood.
The Valley Striders Athletic Club organise annual races along the route which are run in April/May.

Bear left with the road as it becomes Cathcart Street (no road sign), to the T-junction with Rampart Road (again no road sign).

Turn right at the T-junction, passing Holborn Approach on your right and continue straight over the crossroads with Woodhouse Street, into Delph Lane (no road sign – Licensed Club to your right).

Go uphill, to pass houses to either side of you and past Providence Avenue and Cliff Terrace, following Delph Lane as it bears slightly to the right and still uphill.
After Inglewood Terrace on the left, the road soon begins to dip downhill, and at the very end of this lane, you reach Woodhouse Ridge, the first of the fingers of parkland.

Turn left into the park by the metal gate, which is next to a low red-brick wall.

Note the information board down to your right, below the railings.

Woodhouse Ridge was once used by Cistercian monks walking from Kirkstall Abbey and this area was also the site of civil war skirmishes.
It was opened for public access in 1846, and developed as a public park in the Edwardian era.
The now derelict bandstand was built in 1905, and it is hoped that this can be restored.

At the end of the metal railings, take the top path, straight ahead (S.P. Meanwood Valley Trail, Dales Way Link).

IGNORE the first metal squeeze-gate on the left and continue straight on (S.P. Dales Way), with a high stone wall to your left. Keep to this main, wide path.

The path soon dips downhill, with an old house and then new flats over to your left, to a metal gate.

Pass through the large boulders on the right and go through the wooden railings immediately ahead.

Take the left of two footpaths immediately ahead of you (S.P. Meanwood Valley Trail, Dales Way Link and Grove Lane), soon dropping diagonally downhill into woodland.

A path in a gulley soon crosses your way. Cross over it via the steps and carry straight on down a tree-lined path to the rear of houses.

Cross Grove Lane with care, and then go straight on along the tarmac path with a low stone wall to your left, passing a pond on your right, and then alongside Meanwood Beck.

Keep to the tarmac path past houses and the bottom of local streets (yellow way-markers).

Cross Stonegate Road and go into Highbury Lane, past the houses on either side.

At the end of this Lane, take the footpath ahead of you, to pass the old mills on your right.

A medieval corn-mill once stood here, which belonged to Kirkstall Abbey.
Later premises were built on the site as a tannery in the late 18th century and these later became a paper-mill, but this was burnt down in 1852.
Samuel Smith the Younger built the present mills shortly afterwards, but he moved to Tadcaster to found his brewing empire there.
The mills returned to being a fellmongers in 1914, until their closure in 1994.
A fellmonger is an Old English word meaning a person who separates wool from a skin in preparation for tanning.
The mills were converted to flats after that date.

Turn left with the path at the rear of these old mills, at the electricity sub-station. The mill pond appears to your right.

Just after the mill pond, turn right (S.P. Meanwood Valley Trail and Dales Way) down the path. There are allotments to the left and right of this path.

As you approach the corner of a curved estate road, turn right by the standing stone, (S.P. public footpath and Dales Way), and cross over a stone bridge.

Walk along the paved path alongside the beck and cross a metal-railed, concrete bridge. Immediately at the other side of the bridge, go left through a gap in the wall, (S.P. Meanwood Valley Trail and Dales Way) to enter Meanwood Park.

Follow the obvious path ahead and in 100 metres, go straight on at a cross-road of paths (S.P. Meanwood Valley Trail), now on a tarmac path.

Pass the first stone bridge on your left and take the second bridge over Meanwood Beck (S.P. Meanwood Valley Trail).

The path now bears right alongside the beck. Keep to the beck-side path and cross the single-arched stone packhorse bridge.

The elegant and ancient Packhorse Bridge over Meanwood Beck is a Grade II listed structure.

Once over the bridge, turn left (S.P. Meanwood Valley Trail), immediately on reaching the other side.

Pass through the stone arch ahead and turn left.

Hustlers Row, on your right, is a row of twenty cottages, built by a local quarry owner. He used stone from the quarry in their construction, and used them to house his workforce.
There were 106 people living in them in 1871, according to the census survey, an average head count per house of more than five people.

Cross the wooden footbridge (S.P. Meanwood Valley Trail), and turn right once over it (S.P. Meanwood Valley Trail and Dales Way), to enter Hollies Park along a dirt track.

The Hollies is a 14 acre botanical garden with native and exotic tree species.
It is a public park renowned for glorious displays of rhododendrons, which are at their best from May to June. There are also two National Plant Collections here.

Go through the park, with the beck to your right and up a short incline. Go right to cross a stone bridge, with a man made goit to your left. Continue along this path.

Goit is an old Yorkshire word meaning an artificial channel of water.
Its most common use is that of a channel used for feeding a water supply to a mill.

IGNORE the path over the bridge and up to the left (S.P. Hollies) to carry straight on along the raised footpath (S.P. Meanwood Valley Trail).

Cross the wooden bridge to the right, above a waterfall. Go straight on for 20 metres, up the steps ahead and turn to the left, passing through a gate by a stone wall (Meanwood Valley Trail, green and yellow way-marker). The path is now a dirt one.

The beck is now on your left.

Pass through a metal squeeze gate to enter Smith Mills Lane (no road sign), and turn left (blue and yellow way-marker).
Cross the Lane to walk on the right hand side, uphill, past buildings on your right.

Just before the dual carriageway of the A.6120 Outer Ring Road, turn right down a tarmac, tree-lined drive which, in a few metres, becomes a stony footpath.
This path travels parallel to the A.6120, with a line of trees to your left.

Travel through the underpass on your left, by Adel Beck, to pass under the A.6120, Outer Ring Road.

At the other side, turn immediately right, up the steps, following the footpath beside Adel Beck. This is Scotland Wood.

As the path splits at the site of a ruined mill, and with large boulders to your right, take the left hand, upper path. (S.P. public footpath and Dales Way).

Scotland Mill, the remains of which are to your right, was built in 1785 for processing flax into linen. Seven cloth-workers' cottages were also built on site.
A dam and a huge water wheel were constructed to power it.
The mill was acquired by John Marshall and Samuel Fenton several years later, with a view to converting it into a cotton processing mill.
It was quickly realised that the premises were too small and in 1791, John built the six-storey Marshall Mills in Holbeck, Leeds.
This mill employed 2,000 workers and was said to be the largest factory in the world. His son then built the famous Temple Mills nearby, in the Egyptian style.
This mill had the largest single room in the world (2 acres) and had a grass roof to maintain humidity for the flax. Sheep even grazed on the rooftop.
The world's first mechanical lift was invented here – to get the sheep on and off the roof! Scotland Mill was converted to a paper mill and was used up to the 1850s.
It was burned down in 1906 and abandoned.
The cottages lasted a little longer.
The retting pits (for soaking flax) and foundations are all that remain and the site has become overgrown.

Continue along the well defined footpath to the top-side of woodland and over a small stone slab footbridge above a tiny stream, which may be dry (Meanwood Valley Trail way-marker).

As the path splits again, take the left, upper rocky path (way-marks painted in yellow on trees) and continue along the path to the top side of the wood, alongside fields to your left.

Where the seven arches viaduct with it's grey metal railings comes into view on your right, the path splits yet again. Take the right hand path slightly downhill towards the viaduct and IGNORE the path and the large white arrow painted on a tree to your left.

The Seven Arches viaduct at the top end of Scotland Wood is more correctly an aqueduct, since it carried drinking water from Eccup reservoir to the city of Leeds. It was built at the end of the 1830s and is connected to Eccup reservoir, 1.3 miles away, by a hidden underground tunnel, known as Blackmoor Tunnel.
The tunnel and aqueduct proved unable to cope with increasing demand and was only fully used for 24 years, becoming redundant by 1861.
New pipelines and conduits now meet modern requirements.

Take this right hand path to pass down the slope immediately to the left of the viaduct.

At the end of the arches, turn left (yellow way-marker on bridge parapet).

Go through the trees, uphill (yellow painted way-markers on trees and boulders).

Once the path has levelled out, follow it slightly downhill (yellow way-marker on tree to the left). Keep on this main path through the trees. It soon starts to go slightly uphill again and passes an old stone gatepost on the left.

Twenty metres further on, the 'Slabbering Baby' on the right is a natural spring and is of medieval origin. The square stonework surrounding it is probably Victorian and the spring takes it's name from the carved head in the stonework.

Go straight ahead, ignoring small paths to the left and right to pass over a small stone bridge over a stream (yellow way-marker), and up the steps at the other side, passing a small pond on your left. Go over a small wooden bridge at the top side of the pond. Pause here.
IGNORE the footpath straight ahead and turn immediately right, over a second small wooden footbridge (yellow way-marker on tree), and up the rocky footpath going uphill.

Bear left with the path when you come to white wooden fencing which surrounds cricket and rugby pitches (yellow way-markers on trees).

Now keep to the main footpath through the trees, ignoring a smaller path to the right after the pitch.

IGNORE the footpath down to the left (S.P. public footpath) and continue slightly uphill as the path becomes flanked with holly bushes.

Emerge into a picnic site clearing. IGNORE the wooden fingerpost by the picnic tables (S.P. public footpath) and pass by the standing stone (S.P. Meanwood Valley Trail), going left.

Go through the next set of gateposts and fencing, into and through a small car park and the metal arch at the other side.

Go directly across Stairfoot Lane and follow the path uphill to the right, through trees (S.P. public bridleway).

At the metal gate, IGNORE the first wooden signpost (public bridleway), go past the metal gate and turn right along the field side (S.P. public bridleway), slightly uphill.

Leeds/Bradford International Airport, seen in the distance to your left, began as a private air club in 1931, with the first scheduled passenger flights some four years later. At the start of World War II, Avro built an aircraft factory next to the airport and the runway was used to test military aircraft.
Mock farm buildings were built around it and the roof of the factory was painted green. Papier-mache cows, sheep and even a duck pond were placed on the roof to avoid enemy detection from the air.
This factory produced Bristol Blenheim and Lancaster bombers as well as the Anson, York and Lincoln aircraft.
Civil flights resumed in 1947 and the airport continued to develop and expand. It currently carries 3 million passengers per year and there are further expansion plans. It is the highest airport in England and often operates when others cannot.

At the field corner, carry on straight ahead, along the bridleway.

The golf course seen to your left is that of Headingley Golf Club, which was formed in 1892. The Club moved to this site in 1906.
Golfing giants such as Harry Vardon and Henry Cotton have played competitively here. The course lies on the site of a Roman settlement dating from the early fifth century. In 1969, a Roman road was discovered, which travels across the course, and the 3rd, 12th, 14th and 15th fairways.

As you reach the road, King Lane (no road sign), we leave the Meanwood Valley Trail here.
Continue straight across King Lane (S.P. public footpath), to the right of a white painted house.
Go through or around the metal gate and go straight ahead.
A golf practise area appears to your left.

Go down the path ahead, with the hedge-line to your left.
This is the first taste of really open countryside since we left Leeds City Square.

Cross over a stile ahead of you (green and yellow way-marker) and continue straight ahead along the fence-line.

Continue to the next stile at the field and fence corner and turn left over it (S.P. Dales Way Link, green and yellow way-marker).

Travel in a straight line along the path to pass over two stiles next to woodland (S.P. public footpath, Dales Way Link).
Eccup Reservoir is on your right.

Eccup reservoir was constructed in 1843, and was enlarged in later years. It provides drinking water for the citizens of Leeds. It is the largest area of water in West Yorkshire. During the drought of 1995, thousands of tankers of water had to be brought in from Northumberland and Goole to keep supplies at an acceptable level.
A pipeline now exists between the East and West of the district to ensure no reoccurrence. Parts of the surrounding areas are S.S.S.I. (Sites of Special Scientific Interest) for wild flowers.

After the second stile, cross up and over the open field, along the well defined path and then into Eccup Moor Road, via a stile next to a metal gate.

Turn right along this road.

To the left, on the horizon, lies Bank Top Lane.
It is thought to be part of a Bronze Age ridge-way, which once ran between Ireland and Europe. It is still walked today, as part of the Ebor Way.

Keep right at the 'V' road junction (name plate, Village Road, on the left) and walk past the 'dead end' sign on the left.

To this point, the White Rose Way has, for the most part, followed the line of the Dales Way Leeds link.
The link now sweeps away to our left to Ilkley where the official Dales Way starts. The Dales Way is an 82 mile walk, taking in the Wharfe valley, Ribblehead and on to Sedburgh, and Staveley, before ending at Bowness on Windermere in the Lake District.

Fifty metres after the 'V' junction and just before Bank House Farm, as the road swings right, take the track to the left side of the farm, (S.P. public bridleway and Leeds Country Way owl sign on a post).
This becomes a concreted drive.

Keep straight on, along a path to the left of the wall, as the drive turns to the right, into the farm.

Carry straight on past a metal gate as the path becomes hedged at each side.

At a stile on the left, the Leeds Country Way comes in to join our route for a short way. Its way-markers are yellow owls on a green background).

The Leeds Country Way is a 62 mile circular walk around the city of Leeds.
It was adopted by the Countryside Unit of West Yorkshire Metropolitan County Council and brought into use in the 1980s.
It was adapted and updated in 2006.

IGNORE this stile, our route goes straight ahead and bends to the right in 30 metres.

Follow this hedged track to walk along the right side of woodland and turn left through the centre of the wood (S.P. Leeds Country Way), on the path.

As you emerge from the wood, turn right (S.P. bridleway and Leeds Country Way), to walk alongside the wood, before turning left with the path in 150 metres.

Continue to the field end, passing a wooden post at the end of the hedgerow and go straight ahead, still on the same path.

As you reach a track in the dip, turn right (S.P. bridleway and Leeds Country Way) and walk on, with a hedgerow to your right, to reach a T-junction of tracks.

Turn left, (S.P. Leeds Country Way), along the well surfaced track.
IGNORE tracks to the right and left, crossing Stub House Beck and go uphill.

The 'village' seen to your right, does not exist officially. It is not marked on maps.
The fictional village of Emmerdale stars as the setting for the long running television series, which has been on our screens since 1972.
Originally entitled Emmerdale Farm, the early outdoor locations for filming included Arncliffe, Leathley, and later, Esholt.
The nearby town of Otley also features, as the town of Hotten.
In 1998, this purpose built outdoor set was constructed on land belonging to the Harewood House Estate.
It is said to have been modelled on Esholt, but the grid reference 981674, seen on the village's fingerpost sign, relates to the village of Conistone near Kilnsey, in the Yorkshire Dale of Littondale.
The series takes its name from Amerdale, which is the old name for Littondale.
The 'village' is a temporary structure for planning permission purposes and is reviewed every ten years. This area is private, but can be seen to the right, from the track.
Buildings to the left of the track are also used in the series.

Pass Stub House Farm on your left.
The house name on the gate is 'Holdgate Farm', but this is for television purposes.

Walk straight on. You are now entering the Harewood House Estate.

By 1890, the Red Kite bird of prey had been persecuted to extinction, in England and Wales. These birds are largely carrion feeders.
Under a 1999 conservation programme, Red Kites were re-established at Harewood and have become widespread over Yorkshire.
This is now a self sustaining initiative as the birds have spread far and wide.
The birds are now a common sight. They have a distinctive forked tail, and chestnut brown wings, with white flashes underneath.
They have a magnificent five and a half foot wingspan and are masters of soaring and gliding.

As the track drops down to the left of a long stone wall, take the second left path, following the blue and yellow way-markers DOWN the slope.

DO NOT take the first path to the left, which is on the level.

The Leeds Country Way leaves us here, as it goes to the right.

Turn to the right at the bottom of this slope in 50 metres, at a T-junction of paths.

Our route now coincides with the Ebor Way, albeit in the opposite direction to the way it is usually tackled.

The Ebor Way was developed in the 1970s, as a 70 mile long distance footpath.
It runs from Helmsley on the North Yorkshire Moors, via York, Tadcaster, and Wetherby to Ilkley.
By continuing along the Dales Way, it is possible to walk from Helmsley, on the North York Moors, to the Lake District.

Follow this track as it bears downhill and then left (S.P. public bridleway and Ebor Way). Go through the wooden gate (S.P. public bridleway) to pass Carr House on your right.

Harewood House is just visible from here, straight ahead of you.

Continue straight ahead with woodland to your left and a large lake to your right.

Harewood House was built between 1759 and 1771, for the Lascelles family, who are mentioned in the Domesday Book as coming from the village of Loucelles in France at the time of the Norman Conquest, and who still occupy it today.
The Domesday Book was a great survey of England, by officials of King William I and it was compiled around 1086.
This book sought to create a record of the values of land for taxation purposes and to identify land belonging to the Crown.
The book's name came about because its judgement was said to be as final as doomsday.
The grounds were landscaped by Lancelot 'Capability' Brown over nine years from 1772 to 1781.
Streams were dammed, a valley flooded, vast quantities of earth moved and plantations created. He was paid £6,000 for this work.
Many rooms of the house served as a convalescent hospital in the two World Wars.
The house contains important collections of furniture and paintings whilst the grounds are home to an extensive Bird Garden.

Both are open to the public, as are the many events held throughout the year. George Henry Hubert Lascelles, the 7th Earl of Harewood, and first cousin to Queen Elizabeth II, died here in July 2011, aged 88 years. His son succeeds to the title.

The track swings to the left at the bottom of the slope (S.P. public bridleway) and continues to the right, through metal gates (Ebor Way way-marker) and past high-walled gardens to your right.

After the walled gardens, bear left (S.P. public bridleway), then right on a tarmac lane, with a low stone wall to your right.

Pass a stone house on your left, near the bottom of the hill.

At the triangle of tracks just after the house, bear left, then straight on and over a stream via the stone bridge ahead.
Go up the hill on the concrete track, through the wooden gate and straight ahead, to the left of the buildings known as Harewood Yard.

There is a history board outside it. (S.P. bridleway and Ebor Way).

Go up the hill on the broad tarmac track to pass through a metal gate and cattle grid at the top of the hill. The track is now a concreted drive through a deer park.

As the drive reaches a triangle of tracks, take the tarmac track to the right and travel up the hill (S.P. public bridleway).

The track levels out (viewpoint bench here!). At the tree-line ahead, go through the metal gate next to the cattle grid.

IGNORE the footpath sign and track to your left and go straight on along the tarmac drive.

After the cattle grid, it becomes a walled drive.
Walk on, to pass through the wooden gate at the end of the drive, and straight ahead into the village of Harewood as the drive becomes Church Lane.

Harewood village is largely clustered around All Saint's church and prior to 1096, land in this area was granted to the de Rumily family, who came to Britain after the Norman Conquest.
Contrary to popular belief, the Normans were not purely French, but were actually descended from the Scandinavian Viking invaders of France.
The Vikings were granted the region of Normandy by the French King in A.D. 911. Over successive generations, they successfully integrated with the people of that region.

Continue straight ahead to the main A.61 Leeds to Harrogate Road.

For those who have chosen to overnight at Harewood, accommodation may be found just to the right.

The frequent 36 bus from bus-stops outside the pub, serves Leeds and Harrogate.

Harewood to Linton (7.0 miles, 11.3 km)

For the remainder, turn left along the pavement alongside the A61.
IGNORE the first public footpath off to the right (S.P. public footpath), opposite Bondgate, and continue along the pavement.

50 metres past this footpath, as the pavement on the left side of the road comes to an end, cross the road, taking great care.

Keep going to the left, on the tarmac pavement, alongside the A.61.

As the A.61 swings quite sharply to the left downhill, take the track on the bend, to the right of the crash-barriers, signposted 'Ebor Way'. (rickety sign, sometimes lying in the grass). A further sign on the right reads 'Harewood Estate. Private Property. No Parking'.

Harewood Castle, seen amongst the woods to the left behind the high stone wall, was built in 1366, being a castellated manor house. It has long been in a ruined state.

Follow this track, locally known as Fitts Lane, as it heads downhill.

Pass over a stile next to a gate (yellow way-marker) and continue down the hill, passing a strip of woodland on your left.

IGNORE the track which goes at right angles off to the right, to carry straight on along the track, (green and yellow way-marker) with trees and bushes on either side.

Further down the track, Almscliffe Crag, seen as a rocky outcrop 90 degrees to the left on the horizon, was formed when shale and mud around it eroded at a faster rate than the millstone grit it is composed of. It has a number of graded climbing routes for enthusiasts.

The downhill path reaches the River Wharfe at the bottom of the hill. Turn right alongside it, to follow the green lane.

The River Wharfe is around 80 miles long, originating at Beckermonds in the Yorkshire Dales National Park.
It flows through Kettlewell, Grassington, Bolton Abbey, Ilkley, Otley, Wetherby and Tadcaster, and is tidal for the last ten miles below Tadcaster weir.
It joins the River Ouse at Cawood.
The river's name has Celtic origins, which means twisting or winding.
A stone bearing the image of the Roman Goddess Verbeia was found in the Wharfe at Ilkley. She is regarded as the goddess of the river.
The stone may be seen in All Saints Parish Church in Ilkley.
More than 230 different species of birds have been observed along the Wharfe valley.
Otters are known to have colonised this stretch of the river up to Collingham.

Follow the well defined green lane along the riverside all the way around a huge field. Continue alongside the river past a gateway (green and yellow way-marker).

Harewood Hill Speed Climb, seen up to your right, is a motorsport venue where

enthusiasts attempt to drive from the bottom of the hill course to the top, in the fastest time.
An enthusiast bought Stockton Farm and allowed the club to develop the land. The first meeting was held in September 1962, with a national event the following year. It is firmly on the motorsport calendar to this day.

Keep to the riverside, go over a stile and after the second stile, enter Carthick Wood.

BEWARE as the path is very near to the riverbank, which can overhang in places.

Around 200 metres into the wood, IGNORE the small path off at 45 degrees to the right and continue along the main riverside path.

This path exits the wood and becomes a river and field-side path. Keep to the left, beside a large field to your right and with the tree-line to your left.

As the river turns sharply left, and a line of woodland is immediately in front of you, sight the wooden marker post with yellow top directly ahead, and take the path at the side of this post, into the woodland (green and yellow way-marker).

Cross a small stream (may be dry at certain times) and follow the footpath to the left.

Enter the tree-lined gully uphill, passing a yellow top marker post (green and yellow way-marker). Go straight up this gully. Go straight on through fencing near the top of the gully, still uphill.

The gully soon bears left and emerges into the open at a yellow top marker post (green and yellow way-marker). Enter a second tree lined gully straight ahead.

At the top of the gully, pass over a stile (yellow top marker post,) then a second stile to reach Harewood Avenue, the A.659.

BE AWARE that this road can be busy and grass verges slippery.

Turn left here and cross the road to the right side verge.

Prior to the sign for East Keswick Plant Centre, re-cross the road to walk along the left side verge.

It is necessary to cross again, to the verge on the right after the 'staggered junction' road sign, for safety reasons.

Crabtree Lane joins the A.659 from the right, next to a small car park.

Turn down the track to the left (S.P. public bridleway), opposite this road junction, crossing the roads with care once more.

Pass to one side of a metal gate, continuing down the bridlepath (blue and yellow way-marker), to rejoin the river at the bottom of the hill.

Follow the riverside bridleway sign along the well-defined track, passing to the right of a metal gate.
The track swings a little away to out to the right, IGNORE the gate, stile and steps up to the right, and the stile down to the right of the bridge, to cross the river by Woodhall Bridge.

Woodhall Bridge, is of iron and timber construction and bears the name of the makers, Joseph Whitham and Son, Leeds, and is dated 1868 (pictured).
The Perseverance Iron Foundry was created by John Whitham, on Kirkstall Road in Leeds, opposite to where the Radio Aire Studios now stand.
John died in 1823, but he had involved his family in the trade.
He left the business in the hands of his sons, Joseph and Stephen.
Joseph and his own son ran the business from 1850 to 1885, when it was sold.
Stephen founded Monk Bridge Iron Works, further up Kirkstall Road.

Follow the path as it goes slightly uphill, past Spring Wood on your left.

Carry on uphill and through a gate, to pass a high wall to your right.

Shortly afterwards, at a T-junction of paths, turn right to enter a wood via a gate

Go straight ahead, but in around 100 metres, follow the diverted, fenced bridleway down to the right (S.P. New Bridle Path and Nature Walk).

It shortly joins a tarmac drive, carry straight on, then to the left, as it curves uphill.

Pass the Carmelite Monastery on the left.

The Carmelites arrived in England in 1242, from Mount Carmel in Palestine.
They accompanied the nobles returning from the Crusades.
The building to the left, now a monastery, was purchased by the Diocese of Leeds in 1966, and the Carmelite silent order of nuns was established there in 1969.
It is still used for that purpose today.
The monastery has been visited by Mother Theresa of Calcutta.

The tarmac drive emerges at the rear of Wood Hall Spa Hotel.

A 'vavasour' was a person who held lands obtained from the local lord, as distinct from the King. This title became a family name in Britain after 1066.
Wood Hall Hotel and Spa was originally built as a home for the local Vavasour family, in 1750. The Hall became a boy's preparatory school in 1935.
Famous alumni include the Yorkshire and England cricketer, Sir Len Hutton.
The building was converted to a small luxury hotel in 1988, with a Spa extension added in 1992. It is part of the Small Luxury Hotels of the World Group.

At the far, rear corner of the Hotel, and just before the car park, the path turns left, (S.P. bridleway, blue and yellow way-marker).

The path is level at first, then travels uphill through Lime Kiln Wood to Springfield House, Woodhall Cottage and West View, all private houses, on the left.

At the driveway to West View, at the top of the hill, turn 90 degrees to your right and take the track to your right (S.P. public bridleway, blue and yellow way-marker). In about 200 metres the track bears to the right and drops gently downhill, becoming a footpath and into the top side of woodland (green and yellow way-marker).

The path emerges from the wood, to continue along the edge of it.

Bear left with the path along the edge of the wood and then right at the end of it, to pass between gateposts.

Turn left immediately after the gateposts (public bridleway way-marker), along the field edge, to a large tree ahead of you.

At the tree, turn right with the path and go straight across the field, heading for a copse of trees.

Take the fenced path through the copse straight ahead.

The path emerges onto a tarmac lane, which is Trip Lane. Follow this to the left.

Collingham village, seen in the valley down to the right, was the 'village of Cola's folk' and by 1167, it was known as Collinegham.
St.Oswald's church, in the village, was founded by Saxons and rebuilt by the Normans. During restoration in the 1840s, a seventh century Saxon cross was discovered in the walls of the church, bearing a Runic inscription which translates as, 'Aenfled set this up in the memory of her cousins Oswy and Oswini King. Pray for their souls'. A second, later cross, showing images of Christ and his Apostles was also uncovered. The crosses are displayed in the church.
Also in the church is a heavy round stone with eight holes, known as a cresset stone. These holes were filled with oil and lit to provide lighting for the congregation. It is one of only three in Yorkshire churches.
The Half Moon village pub, is where Oliver Cromwell spent the night after the Battle of Marston Moor (2nd July 1644), during the first English Civil War.

Follow Trip Lane all the way into the village of Linton.

Linton to Wetherby (1.8 miles, 2.9 km)

At the T-junction in the village, adjacent to the Windmill Public House, turn left,

The Windmill Inn, dates back to the 14th century, and was the home of the owner of the long disappeared village windmill. It was a coaching inn by the 18th century. The pear tree in the yard was grown from seed brought back from the Napoleonic Wars (1799 – 1815).
The inn is a popular pub and restaurant today.

Cross the road, to walk on the right-hand side of the road, downhill.

IGNORE Northgate Lane on the left in 50 metres, to continue along the main road to pass Linton Memorial Hall on your right.

Beware of traffic, and stick to verges where possible, as the road winds uphill and then levels out. Swap to the left side path/verge when the verge on the right runs out.

Cross and walk on the right side verge when the verge on the left runs out, and then back to the left path when possible.

Pass the private road named The Ridge, on the left, and at the dip in the road ahead, opposite a house named Spring Hill, take the footpath (S.P. public footpath) immediately on the right, through the trees, down the steps and onto Wetherby golf course.

BEWARE of flying golf balls and always give way to golfers. RING THE BELL.

Walk across the clearly defined path (S.P. public footpath and Ebor Way), 20 metres to the right of the stream on the left. Head for the big, square blue board ahead of you and pass through the stone arched tunnel in the former railway embankment.

This land, referred to as Scaur Bank or the Ings, held the first recorded Linton steeplechase meeting in 1842.
When the land owner put up the rent substantially, it was decided to seek an alternative site and vacant land was secured at York Road, to the north-east of Wetherby, where the racecourse is to this day.

Once through the tunnel, bear half left (S.P. public footpath and Ebor Way). White boards mark the way ahead.

Wetherby Golf Club was founded as a nine-hole golf course by a group of enthusiasts in 1910, on former steeplechase land.
It was extended to a full eighteen-hole course in the 1920s, by the famous golf course architect, Dr. Alistair Mackenzie.
It is home to a substantial modern clubhouse and golf shop, seen up to your left.

Continue across the course, passing through a hedge archway, through a wooden squeeze stile and then over a stone slab stile, (green and yellow way-marker), into playing fields, with the river Wharfe to your right.

Follow the tree-lined tarmac footpath straight ahead and then cross over the river on the green painted arched footbridge. On reaching the far bank, turn left, and walk along the riverbank path, which curves slowly around to the right.

The small stone building to your left on the far bank, at the apex of the curve, is a rare surviving example of a Georgian cold-bath house, and it is fed by a hillside spring.
It was built in the 18th century and contains a cold plunge bath in the basement and a 'warming room' with fireplace, on the upper floor.
Doctors recommended this treatment as a cure for just about everything, from headaches to impotence.
It is said that the isolated location of many of these bath houses led to them becoming popular places for illicit liaisons.
It was restored in the 1990s and in 2004, the woodland behind was filled with plants and bushes of the period.

You will reach the car park of the Sports Centre via a metal gate.

Note the gravel pitches just to your right at this gate. These are pitches for the French sport of petanque, also known as boules or bocce.
There are very few of these pitches in the U.K.
Wetherby Sports Centre has a very active group of participants, however, and the town is twinned with Privas in the south of France, with regular exchange visits taking place.

Turn left along the footpath adjacent to the drive, to reach Wetherby High Street and its ancient stone bridge.

A bridge over the River Wharfe in Wetherby dates back to medieval times and a substantial structure was certainly known to exist by 1235.
The bridge was restored in 1733 and the six-arch bridge dates from 1824.
Remains of earlier bridges may be seen underneath the arches.
It is now a Grade 2 Scheduled Ancient Monument.
The artist JMW Turner (1775 – 1851) painted and sketched more than seventy Yorkshire scenes in his lifetime and he visited Wetherby, in August 1816.
He produced a well known sketch of the existing bridge, which is in the Tate Gallery in London.
There is an information board about this and the Turner Trail down to the right of the bridge, in the Wilderness car park, by the river.

Turn left over the river bridge.

A water mill has existed on the far bank of the bridge, down to the left, since before 1221. It was used to grind corn and rape-seed.
The mill was later used as a saw-mill, but this was burnt to the ground in 1944.
The huge cog wheel from the mill was found in the mud of the river in 1991 and was restored to its original location in 1993 (pictured).
Salmon steps were created at the far bank in 1871 and the weir renovated in 1982.

Wetherby town centre is ahead of you.

Artefacts from Neolithic and Bronze Age times have been found in the Wetherby area, and the town was also once an important Roman settlement.
In 1086, the town was known as Wedrebi, meaning 'sheep farm'.
There are hints of an ancient castle which overlooked the medieval bridge and a nearby old street, up to the left, is called Castlegate.
The historic Thursday market was granted a Royal Charter in 1240. The market is still operational and thriving today.
The town was sacked and burned by the Scots in 1318/19, in the years after the battle of Bannockburn.
Wetherby developed as a staging post on the important Edinburgh to London route and the first recorded mail-coach arrived in 1786.
At one time in the coaching era, the town boasted 40 inns and ale-houses.
The town is 198 miles equidistant from these capital cities.
The old A.1 trunk road (The Great North Road) ran across the ancient river bridge and right through the centre of the town, until bypassed in 1959.
Wetherby is now largely a commuter town for nearby conurbations and has won many UK and European awards for its beautiful floral displays.

Wetherby to Boston Spa (3.1 miles, 5.0 km)

Whilst still on the bridge (pictured), cross over the road to the right hand side of High Street, taking extra care, if near the mini-roundabout.

Turn right immediately after the bridge end, into Bridge Foot. Do not turn right into the car park unless seeking out the Turner Trail board, carry straight on up the hill, bearing left with the road as it turns in 100 metres.

After the Fire Station, turn right into Walton Road and walk straight ahead, crossing the road to the left hand pavement.

After passing Fourth Avenue, you come to a roundabout. Pass to the left side of it and continue straight ahead, over the top of the A.1 (M) via the road bridge.

Wetherby Racecourse, just over to the left, is the only course in Yorkshire to offer nothing but National Hunt jump meetings.
It is open all year round and is known as the 'Cheltenham of the North'.
Having relocated from Linton, the track opened at Easter 1891 and the first grandstand followed in 1906. Terracing was not added until the 1930s.
It was used as a hospital in World War I, and as an army camp in World War II.
From 1924 to 1963, the course even had its own railway line and station.
Raceday Specials were very popular, bringing punters to meetings from the industrial centres of Yorkshire.
Further stands were added in the 1960s, 70s and in 2000.

In 100 metres, at the signpost 'River Wharfe, Bramham', cross the road and turn right down the bridleway. This soon runs parallel to the A.1 (M).

Turn left 90 degrees, at the first track you come to (S.P. Heuthwaite Lane), with the buildings of Park Hill Farm ahead to your left.
This is a hedged green lane.

On approaching the buildings, at a metal gate, the track turns sharp right (S.P. Ebor Way) and soon sharp left, along Heuthwaite Lane.

Follow this lane for 500 metres to its junction with a tarmac lane, Watersole Lane.

Take the footpath, a grassy track, directly opposite this junction (S.P. public footpath – and with a green and yellow way-marker on an electricity pole), straight ahead into the field, for another 500 metres, passing by the top of a wood.

The path then turns to the right, past a disused stile (green and yellow way-marker, Ebor Way) and alongside the wood at the side of the River Wharfe.

On reaching the woods edge, go straight ahead (S.P. Ebor Way, green and yellow way-marker), along the track at the rear of Flint Mill Grange farm buildings.
Go straight ahead, to the left of the main buildings, along this track.

Flint Mill Grange, and the associated mill by the riverside, began life as a house and water- powered corn-mill, around 1772.
They were built by the Green family, partners in Hartley, Greens & Co., otherwise known as the Leeds Pottery Company of Hunslet, Leeds. This company was founded in 1770. Pierced cream-ware or Leeds-ware, as it became known, was sold throughout Europe, America and Russia.
At its height, the company had 150 highly skilled employees.
Ground flint was used to whiten the clay and to make it more pliable for moulding into pottery.
When the company windmill was severely damaged, the work of grinding the flint was transferred here.
Flint was transported by boat from the south coast of England, via, the English Channel, the North Sea, the Humber, the Ouse and the Wharfe as far as Tadcaster. From here the flint was transported to the mill by horse and cart, for grinding.
The ground flint was then delivered to Hunslet, again by horse and cart, twice weekly. With the demise of the Leeds Pottery Company and the demolition of the factory in 1881, this mill reverted to grinding corn and oats.
The mill ceased operations in 1954 and fell into ruin.
It was converted to a private house in 1975.
Leeds-ware was revived by Leeds City Council in 1983, but the venture was later sold into private hands and is still made today, but in Staffordshire.
The company producing it, in a tribute to the founders, adopted the name of Hartley, Greens & Co.
Original pieces of Leeds-ware are highly prized today.
The pattern books of Leeds Pottery Company may be seen in Leeds Central Library.

This tarmac lane curves down to the right in 100 metres – IGNORE this turn and go straight ahead up the stony track.

The track soon turns sharp right towards woodland and then bears left, alongside the fenced-in woodland to your right.

As you leave the woodland, the track bears slowly to the right and then sharp left by metal and wooden gates with 'private woods' and 'keep out' notices.

The track soon joins a tarmac lane, Wood Lane.

Turn right down the lane (S.P. Ebor Way and Thorp Arch), carrying straight on into and through the village of Thorp Arch.

Keep to the right hand side of the road, and the pavement in the village itself.

Thorp Arch was originally known simply as Thorp, meaning 'village'.
The suffix was derived from the De Arcebus or De Arches family who arrived at the time of William the Conqueror, and who came to own land in this area.
The present bridge over the River Wharfe was built in 1770, near to the old ford and ferry crossing.

Pass the war memorial on the left and the village green and continue straight down this lane, crossing the River Wharfe on the left side pavement, on the road bridge (pictured).

This is Boston Spa.

Previously known as Thorpe Spa, Boston is a Saxon name meaning 'Ox Town'.
It became Boston Spa after John Shires discovered magnesium limestone sulphur springs in 1774. Magnesium sulphate is more commonly known as Epsom Salts.
Spa baths were established and the town became fashionable, until much more plentiful and stronger sulphur springs were discovered in Harrogate.
One of Boston's spas declared bankruptcy in the 1850s, marking the end of the town's fashionable popularity.
Spring jets can still occasionally be seen bubbling up from the small beach behind the church, when river conditions allow.
The town is predominantly Georgian in character and has many fine houses.
On the taller buildings, the window heights diminish with the status of each storey, thus, the upper floors have shorter windows.

Boston Spa to Tadcaster (5.3 miles, 8.4 km)

At the far bank, 20 metres after crossing the bridge, turn left down the footpath (S.P. public footpath, Riverside Path and Ebor Way), to gain the riverside footpath where you turn right, alongside the river (S.P. public footpath Riverside, Ebor Way).

Follow this easy riverside path past the Spa Bath-houses (pictured).

Wharfedale Hall, on your right, was built as a private residence, but became a school in the 1850s. It is now a Leonard Cheshire Disability Care Home and is Grade II listed.

Continue along this path to the very end of building development on your right.
Pass through a gate stile next to a yellow top post, into open countryside.
Head for a second yellow top post, which is straight ahead. (The path next to the river was diverted in June 2011, due to erosion).

Go over a stream via a two-gate wooden footbridge (green and yellow way-marker).

Rejoin the riverside path.

As you join a stretch of woodland, the river bears sharp left. Continue to follow it through a metal squeeze gate, along the riverside path (S.P. Ebor Way, green and yellow way-marker), then up the steps, and along the bank top. Pass over a short wooden footbridge next to a derelict building and then through a metal squeeze gate.

Pass under the disused railway line.

Thorp Arch Trading Estate, across the other side of the river, was built at the start of World War II, on land which was previously three farms.
It was a Royal Ordnance Factory, making ammunition and bombs for the R.A.F. and Army. It had its own railway sidings and reservoirs.
At its height, there were 619 buildings, many of which were semi-underground, with earth or concrete blast walls surrounding them in order to contain accidental explosions.

Up to 10,000 people, mainly women, were employed here.
It was closed in 1957, and was developed as a retail and small business park in the 1960s.
Many of the original buildings are still in use today.

Rejoin the riverside path.
In around 200 metres, an island can be seen in mid-river, opposite a red-brick cube of a building on the far bank. (The watercourse on the right, separating the island from the main riverbank, may be dry at certain times of the year).

100 metres past this island, cross a stile into a gully.

After the mid-river island, at the river end of the gully, a ford is marked on maps.
This is believed to be St. Helen's Ford, a river crossing point on the extension of the old Roman road from Lincoln to Aldborough, near Boroughbridge.
You are now standing on that Roman Road.
Helen, after whom the ford was named, was the mother of the Emperor Constantine, whose troops served at York.
She is the supposed re-discoverer of the 'True Cross' on which Jesus died.
As a consequence, she was invoked as the finder of lost objects, becoming popular amongst the Celts and Brigantes people.
Numerous springs and wells were dedicated as thanks to St. Helen, chiefly in East and West Yorkshire and in the South-West of England.
The Celts were the people who originally inhabited this area prior to the Romans coming to Britain around 400 B.C. They became part of the Iron Age or Brigante people in Yorkshire.
The Brigantes were fierce warriors who had strongholds at Aldborough (then Isurium Brigantium), Almondbury near Huddersfield, and at the summit of Ingleborough Mountain in the Yorkshire Dales.
Geo-physical surveys at Aldborough in 2011, revealed below ground signatures of a huge, tiered, Roman amphitheatre and an adjacent sports arena at Sudbury Hill.
Aldborough was the civil capital of the Brigantes and it was clearly an important later Roman town too, making the road you are standing on, much more significant than previously thought.
This road, (known officially as Roman Road 280, Rudgate) led further northwards, to Corbridge on Hadrian's Wall.
The Brigantes were finally defeated by the Romans at the Battle of Stanwick, near Scotch Corner, in 76 A.D.

The path takes a sharp right along the gully, leaving the river behind you.

In the field to your left, once stood a Roman fort, used as a base to guard the ford.
The foundations may be seen as ridges in the field, after the first line of hedges.
It may have been known as Langborough.
Measuring 340 x 210 metres, this was a substantial fortification.
Stones from this fort were regularly ploughed up and can be found in many walls and buildings locally.
Simian and Roman pottery, coins, rings and a burial urn have also been recovered here.
Interestingly, many of the coins bear the image of Constantine, the son of Helen.

This tree lined path soon becomes a hedged track.

Continue along this track, passing the single bar metal gate at the end, to reach the A.659 and turn left along this road (S.P. Ebor Way - Along Verge).

The top of this field, to your left, is known as Adaman Graves or Groves. Adaman was the Abbot of Hue or Huensis and who died on 23rd October 704. He lived at Calcaria (Tadcaster) and had connections with religious buildings in Newton Kyme. Little else is known about him.

Turn left at the first road junction you come to, into Croft Lane (S.P. Ebor Way, Newton Kyme), and into the village of Newton Kyme.

IGNORE the roads to the left and the right in the village centre and continue straight on, at the grassy central triangle, towards the church.

Newton Kyme derives it's name from a contraction of 'new town' and the Old English word cymbe, which means (place at) 'the hollow', thus, 'new town at the hollow'. As well as the Roman fort, aerial photographs show evidence of earlier structures, including a henge.
The character of the later buildings is largely Georgian.

Fifty metres past the latter junction, take the footpath into the field on the right, between the stone posts (S.P. Ebor Way, To the Church, public footpath).

Newton Kyme Hall, to your left, was owned by the Fairfax family.
They were descendants of Sir Thomas Fairfax, an outstanding military leader in the English Civil War. He led the New Model Army at the Battle of Naseby, which effectively ended Charles the First's reign.

Pass to the right of the church and the path swings to the left.

The Norman church of St. Andrew is in the grounds of Newton Kyme Hall.
The Venerable Bede, 672 – 735 A.D., was a monk and religious scholar from Northumbria. He is buried in Durham Cathedral, and was later proclaimed a Saint. He completed a History of the Church of England (Historia Ecclesiastica), in A.D. 731, in which he gave an account of Heina, who became the first nun in the Newton Kyme area.
Remains of foundations near to the church are thought to be of her place of residence. In the church is a memorial to Commander Robert Fairfax of the Royal Navy, who was involved in the capture of Gibraltar in 1704. He retired from the Navy in 1711 and later became an M.P. and Lord Mayor of York.

At the end of the church grounds, turn diagonally left to cross the open field, heading for the left hand corner of the woodland ahead.

Kyme Castle, seen back to the left (if tree foliage allows) and to the right of the church, was built as a Manor House in the 13th century and was fortified in the 14th century. Little remains, apart from a rubble wall with an archway and two windows.

This path then rejoins the River Wharfe.
Walk to the right, alongside it and pass through a gate stile (S.P. Ebor Way).

The path now meanders gently alongside the river embankment, following the curves of the river.

From May to September, yellow water lilies (Nuphar lutea) may be seen in the river here. They are also known as spatterdock or cow lilies and are at their best from June. These plants have long been associated with medicinal products. Their roots and seeds were ground up and used in compounds. The seeds were also used to produce flour.

Pass through two metal gates over a small stream (green and yellow way-marker, Ebor Way).

Follow the curves of the riverbank path.

Walk over a fenced, stone bridge over a second stream and turn left once over it (public footpath way-marker). Take care on the stone steps on the way down.

In 100 metres, go through the arched stone tunnel to then pass the flow gauging station building. After this building IGNORE the gravel track up to the right to keep straight on by the riverside.

Pass under the arched, disused railway bridge, which is ahead of you.

The handsome railway viaduct over the River Wharfe was built in 1849, by the celebrated railway engineer, George Hudson. The railway line to York was never completed however.
Instead, lines were laid in 1883, to serve the flour mills on the far bank.
The line closed for freight in 1967.

Pass the weir on your left to go through a wooden gate stile.

After passing the weir, to your right, the remains of a Motte and Bailey castle may be seen. Only the Motte (hill) and ditches remain.
Utilising rubble from an old Roman settlement, the Normans constructed this castle in the 13th century.
In a model of recycling, when this castle was demolished, the stone was then used in the re-construction of the river bridge ahead of you.

Follow the tarmac path, passing the church on your right.

This site has been a place of worship since the 7th century, when a stone cross was the focal point for religious gatherings. Saxon, Norman and medieval remains have been found in the current St. Mary's church, which was substantially rebuilt by the Victorians in 1877, due to flood damage of the previous building.
A stained glass roundel is incorporated into the present windows. This roundel dates to medieval times and features St. Catherine, the patron saint of linen weavers, which was then an important trade in the town.

Pass a single row of Georgian houses to your right, all the way to the stone road bridge in Tadcaster, and the A659.

It is believed that the first river crossing in Tadcaster was built by the Romans and was of timber construction. A fort defended this position.
By 1150, the town was called Tahecastre.
The first stone bridge dates from around 1200 and later, stone from the Motte and Bailey castle was utilised. It has been altered and added to over the years, the present bridge dating from around 1700. Various mason's marks may be seen beneath it.

The Romans founded Tadcaster as Calaria, which is Latin for lime-kilns. This, no doubt, is attributed to the local geology, which is limestone.
The area has long been quarried and stone from here was used to build a Roman fort at York, York Minster, Selby Abbey and many local churches.
Quarrying at Jackdaw Crags quarry continues on a smaller scale, to this day.
Breweries have existed here for centuries, thanks to sulphates-rich springs.
They can be traced from tax returns as far back as 1341.
The first well used exclusively for brewing was sunk in 1758, and is still in use at Samuel Smith's Old Brewery, which is Yorkshire's oldest brewery.
A legal dispute in the 1880s amongst the Smith brewing family led to John Smith's brewery being built next to Samuel Smith's brewery, as separate businesses.
Only three breweries still exist in the town, Samuel Smiths, John Smith's and the Tower Brewery of 1883, now owned by Molton Coors.
Following the demise of the famous Tetley's brewery of Leeds in 2011, Tetley's Smoothflow bitter is now produced here by Molton Coors.
Tetley's cask bitter is now produced in Wolverhampton, much to the chagrin of Yorkshire folk.

Although not strictly on the route, the Ark, a medieval building in the town centre, up to the right and 75 metres along Kirkgate, is worth a viewing, especially if you are staying in the town.
It was built in the late 1500s and was so called because of the carvings of Noah and his family on the corbels.
It is said that the Pilgrim Fathers met here to plan their voyage to the New World.
Over the centuries, it has been a meeting place, an inn, a post office, a butchers, a dwelling house, and is now the offices for the Town Council (pictured).

Tadcaster to Bishopthorpe (7.7 miles, 12.4 km)

Three miles to the south of Tadcaster, at Towton, the bloodiest battle ever to take place on English soil took place on 29th March 1461, in a snowstorm.
It was the sixth year of the War of the Roses between the Houses of Lancaster and York, fought for the right to the English throne.
It is reported that of 50,000 combatants, 28,000 men were killed over a period of ten hours, and that the River Cock turned red with blood.
The Yorkists routed the Lancastrians, and this led to Edward IV displacing Henry VI, as King of England.
It is said that red and white, or 'burnt' roses, grew on the battle-site afterwards.
Shakespeare highlighted this battle in his play, Henry VI, Part III.
A monument was erected at the site in 1929.
Artefacts continue to surface and in 1996, a mass grave was discovered, which contained skeletons with horrific bone injuries.
A further five recently identified mass grave sites were examined in 2011 and 2012.

Turn left on the A.659 along the left side pavement, all the way through the North Eastern half of the town.

Carry straight on up the slight gradient of the A.659, passing the Bay Horse pub (Road-sign A.64 York) and later the Leeds Arms pub on the left and then with open fields to the right.

Pass the last of the houses on the left and continue straight ahead towards the A.64.

Pass the Ford and John Deere garages on your left, towards the A.64 ahead.

After the last building on the left, a bungalow, continue for a short distance along the tarmac path alongside the A.64, then turn left down Catterton Lane, (Road-signed Catteron and Healaugh).

The lane crosses a stream where metal railings are at either side of the lane, and bends to the right, towards a small area of woodland on the left, on the corner of the lane.

As the lane bears left, take the footpath going straight ahead, into the field (S.P. public bridleway and Ebor Way), through a wooden gate then a metal gate. Go to the right of the barbed wire fence.

It will come as no surprise that the straight path we are now following all the way to Bishopthorpe is an old Roman road, called 'The Old Street' (pictured).
It was the major road between York and Tadcaster, the A.64 of its day.
It takes little effort to imagine cohorts of soldiers marching along this road.

The line of this path is arrow-straight and enters a strip of woodland via a metal gate. The path goes straight on through the middle of the woodland. This section can be a little jungle-like with an abundance of nettles in the height of summer, shorts wearers beware!

At the end of the woodland, cross a small stream, (may be dry at certain times) next to a red and white gas pipe-line post and then alongside a man-made water-course on your right. Open fields are to your left.

Keep going straight on, passing a red and white gas-pipe post, over the man made water course and into a second strip of woodland. The water course is now on your left.

As this water course turns 90 degrees to the left, carry straight on as the path soon becomes a wide track.
Pass another red and white gas-pipe post on your right and go straight ahead up the well defined tarmac twin-track.

IGNORE the S.P (public bridleway) on your left by the large oak tree and go straight on, slightly uphill.

The track bears ever so slightly to the right as you reach a small cluster of buildings and a pond, to your left.

Pass through the middle of the buildings and to the right of white-painted cottages, to join the A.64 carriageway.

Keep to the left side footpath (S.P. Ebor Way) to walk alongside the carriageway.

Pass the Travelodge, Little Chef and petrol station on your left.
Take care crossing the access (look behind you) and egress (look to your left) roads.

At this point IGNORE older maps, which direct users of the Ebor Way to cross both carriageways of the A.64, climbing over the central crash barrier.
DO NOT DO THIS UNDER ANY CIRCUMSTANCES.

Keep to left hand pavement and continue to follow the line of the A.64.

IGNORE fingerpost (S.P. public footpath) on left near the large road sign and carry straight on.

At the slip-road (Road-sign Colton, Bilborough Services), cross it with care on the cycle path, looking behind you as you do so, to reach the reservation.

Also cross the slip-road from your left, to go straight ahead towards the bridge.

Take the tarmac path to your left (S.P. Services) and go up the steps onto the bridge.

Turn to the right and cross the bridge over the A.64.

You will see the cooling towers of three power stations ahead, all of which lie on the line of the River Aire.
The first, ahead and just to the right, is Drax Power Station.
This was built between 1974 and 1986, and claims to be the newest, largest, cleanest and most efficient power station in the U.K. It is coal fired and produces 7% of all the U.K's electricity needs. They are currently investigating biomass as a fuel.
The second one, further to the right, is Eggborough Power Station and this was built between 1962 and 1967. It consumes both coal and biomass wood pellets.
The third, further to the right, is Ferrybridge C power station. This stands on the site of two demolished power stations and was opened in 1967. It was the first power station in Europe to achieve 2000MW output. This station is coal, gas and biomass powered. It produces 80% of all co-fired renewable energy in the U.K.

Immediately after crossing the A.64, turn right down the steps at the other side.

Turn left along the service road, passing a small pond on your left, and cross the road you have just dropped down from, as it comes in from your left.

Go down the fenced path (S.P. Ebor Way, public bridleway) to the left.

Travelling in a straight line once again on the old Roman road, cross a small wooden footbridge, (S.P. Ebor Way) in the tree-line ahead.
Go straight on, with a hedge to the left and open fields, to your right.

Botanist Max Hooper came up with a formula for dating hedges which has proved to be remarkably accurate. It has become scientifically accepted as Hooper's Rule. For every thirty yard stretch of hedge, if the number of tree species in it is ten, then it is a thousand years old, eight species – eight hundred years old etc.
Some hedges in the U.K. have been found dating back to Roman times.

Pass alongside several fields on your right.

IGNORE a wooden footbridge on your left which leads into woods and carry straight on (S.P. Ebor Way).

The path reaches a tarmac lane on a corner. Go through the metal gate (S.P. Ebor Way) and into the lane.

Take the tarmac lane to your left, continuing on the straight line of the old Roman road – DO NOT turn down the lane to the right.

IGNORE the S.P. (public bridleway) to your left down a track with a red gate when it appears. Carry straight on along the lane.

Askham Bryan Agricultural College over to the left, started out as the Yorkshire Institute of Agriculture, after the Second World War.
In 1948, the Institute accepted its first students.
It assumed its present name in 1967 and now caters for about 4000 students.
The college supports it's own farm and three others, and has courses in equine, animal and land management, business, food production, engineering and bioscience amongst others.
Alumni include many specialists in their field (see what I did there?), including horticulturalists and broadcasters Geoffrey Smith and Joe Maiden.

Continue along the lane straight ahead until you come to a crossroads at the edge of Copmanthorpe village.

Turn right here (S.P. Village Centre) crossing the road to the left side pavement. Pass Horseman Drive on the left and follow the main road as it swings sharply left into School Lane and Copmanthorpe centre.

Copmanthorpe village centre, lies just south of the old Roman road from York to Tadcaster.
It is shown in the Domesday Book of 1087, as Copemantorp, a Viking name which means trader's or craftsmen's village.
Many of the village streets are named after ancient occupations and trades.
When William the Conqueror became King of England, he raised tax levels, which caused popular uprisings in the North in 1068 and 1069. These were quelled, but William took revenge by burning all villages, crops and herds between the Humber and Durham in the 'Harrying of the North'.
Many villages in this region were shown as 'laid waste' in the Domesday Book, but Copmanthorpe appears to have recovered quickly.
In 1558, Sir Thomas Vavasour was buried at St. Mary's church in Bishophill.

At the T junction (Road-sign Askham Bryan, Tadcaster), turn right past the shopping parade and first left down the one-way street to the left of the Royal Oak pub.

Enter Low Green, going to your left and pass a small grassy green, also on your left.

After Apple Tree Cottage on your right, take the footpath to the right (S.P. public footpath, Ebor Way), passing to the right of an electricity sub-station, down a fenced path.

This path passes school playing fields to your left and then tennis courts and a bowling green on your right.

Turn left at the end of the playing fields, then right (S.P. Ebor Way) to emerge into Wheelwright Close.

Bear right at the end of this short close and follow the curve of the road to the left, passing Sawyer's Crescent, Thatcher's Croft and Ostler's Close.

Turn next right into Fletcher's Croft. Go to the end and turn left along the footpath to the right of domestic garages.

You soon come to the gates at Bishopthorpe Crossing, which is a pedestrian crossing over the main East Coast railway line.

YOU MUST OBSERVE THE PEDESTRIAN TRAFFIC LIGHT SYSTEM HERE AT ALL TIMES.
TRAINS PASS HERE AT UP TO 125 MPH (200KPH).
CROSS ONLY ON A GREEN LIGHT, AND DO SO QUICKLY.
USE THE TELEPHONE PROVIDED IF NO LIGHT IS SHOWING.

Immediately over the railway lines, go to the left down the path (way-markers, public footpath, Ebor Way).

The East Coast Mainline, which you have just crossed, is 393 miles (632km) long and connects London with Edinburgh.
The line passes through Stevenage, Peterborough, Grantham, Newark, Retford, Doncaster, York, Darlington, Durham, Newcastle, Berwick and Dunbar.
To the north of Edinburgh, the line continues to Aberdeen, passing over the iconic red-painted Forth Bridge and the Tay Bridge at Dundee.
The original line was completed in stages between 1846 and 1871 by three separate railway companies.
They combined in 1923 to form the London and North East Railway.
The line has seen classic steam trains run along it, notably the Flying Scotsman and the Mallard, both steam train speed record breakers.
Nowadays, the inter-city expresses travel at speeds up to 125 mph (200kph).

The path then enters fields again, to the left side of a stream and hedge-line (way-marker, public footpath). Keep to the path. Just after a short kink to the left in the footpath, turn right over the stream (way-marker, public footpath).

Follow the well defined path straight ahead, to the right of the hedge-line and electricity pole.
At the end of this hedge, follow another small kink to the left to walk along the right side of a second hedge-line, to the field corner.

Here, the path turns to the right (way-markers, public footpath, Ebor Way), alongside a stream and trees.

In about 50 metres, cross left over the stream by a small footbridge (way-marker, public footpath, Ebor Way) and follow the path as it becomes a tarmac lane past houses on the left, and into the village of Bishopthorpe.

Over the centuries, Bishopthorpe has been variously known as Torp (1086), Thorp-Super-Usam (Thorpe on Ouse) (1194), and Andrewthorpe (1226).
In 1323, it was the host to the 'Great Council' which met here to agree a truce between Edward II and Robert the Bruce.
The aim was to end the raiding of Yorkshire by Scottish clans, subsequent to the Battle of Bannockburn.
It is now a commuter town.

Bishopthorpe to Fulford (3.1 miles, 5.1 km)

IGNORE the first street to the left and the first street to the right, to go straight ahead, passing a small red-brick flower bed.

Here we say a fond farewell to the Ebor Way, which continues into York.

Take the next road on the right, which is Appleton Court (S.P. Trans Pennine Trail, Selby).

The Trans Pennine Trail is a 207 mile multi-user route which links the Irish Sea and the North Sea. It starts at Southport in the west and crosses the north of England to terminate at Hornsea in the east.
There are various loops and spurs to the route, of which York to Selby is one.
The Liverpool to Hull section is part of European Walking Route 8.
The routes are also part of the National Cycle Network.
For the most part, the routes follow disused railway lines and canal towpaths, making the going easier.
The route was started in 1999 and opened in 2001, although not fully completed until 2004, at a cost of £60,000,000.

Bear left at the end of the street, onto the tarmac path on the disused railway line (S.P. Trans Pennine Trail, Selby), and under the road bridge.

The disused railway line between York and Selby features a scale model of the Universe featuring the Sun and the planets, which is some 6.2 miles (9.9km) long. It is also a Sustrans cycle path.

Go straight along this path, passing the Farm Shop to the right.

Keep to the old railway line path, ignoring paths off to the left and right, and following the Selby signposts.

Pass houses to the left and open fields to the right.

Pass Jupiter (How often can you say this on a walk?)

The path crosses over a road at Acaster Bridge.

Travel over the River Ouse via Naburn Bridge.

The sculptures sitting atop Naburn Bridge were funded by the City of York Creative Commission and the National Lottery Fund and were placed there in August 2001. They were chosen by the public and feature a fisherman/woman, a bicycle and a dog. The fishing figure is 4 metres tall and is constructed of galvanised steel.
The title of the work is 'The Fisher of Dreams' (pictured).

The River Ouse is about 55 miles in length, starting from the River Ure at Linton on Ouse and passing through York, Selby and Goole before joining the River Trent at Faxfleet to form the Humber Estuary. It is tidal up to Naburn Locks. The River derives its name from a Celtic word for water. In winter, it is often in flood through the centre of York.

Pass the Marina to your right.

Naburn Marina started life as a boat repair yard in the years after World War Two. By 1963, the operating company turned to the construction of cruisers too, although this was later turned into a retail only operation.
As extra moorings were demanded, the first Marina was excavated in 1971. Expansion continued throughout the 1970s, to its present size of 18 acres.

At the far side of the Marina, leave the Sustrans path and take the fenced cycle path, down to the left (S.P. Fulford).

As you go down this path, Saturn is up to your right (in more ways than one!).

Continue along the cycleway to the left, and parallel to, Naburn Lane.

You soon pass the extensive waste water treatment works on your left on the lane-side footpath.

Continue along this lane and after the last of the water treatment works, at the Fulford road-sign, McArthur Glen Shopping complex appears, to your right, at the other side of the trees.

The York Designer Outlet, seen through the trees to the right, is part of the Europe wide McArthur Glen Group. These premises opened in September 1998 and have over 23,000 square metres of completely indoor retail shopping space.
There are numerous restaurants and cafes.
To the front of the buildings, there is a Park and Ride scheme which operates into York City Centre via Fulford.

At the end of a row of houses on your left, you come to a wooden bus shelter.

A few metres after the wooden bus shelter, at the gap in the hedge (S.P. public footpath), look through the hedges away to the left and Bishopthorpe Palace may be seen across the other side of the River Ouse.
This has been the home of successive Archbishops of York for over 750 years.
When Archbishop Walter De Grey bought the village of Andrewthorpe in 1226, he demolished the old manor house and used some of the stone to erect the palace.
From then on, the village became known as Bishopthorpe (village held by the Bishop).
The ruins of Cawood Castle, destroyed in the English Civil War, were also used as a later source of materials.
New wings were added and the river frontage was completed by 1664.
It was completed in its present form by 1773, with minor work not ceasing until 1900.
It has served as the home of the Archbishops of York from 1241, to the present day.

DO NOT take this path, cross the lane here and continue on the right side footpath, along Naburn Lane.

In 100 metres, as the shopping complex falls away behind you, the lane bears slowly to the right.
Just before the apex, follow the diverted footpath into the field on the left, by-passing metal gates (S.P. public footpath, Fulford, green and yellow way-marker).
(If you have reached Fulford Court on your left as the road rises over the A.64, you have gone 50 metres too far. The public footpath shown here on maps no longer exists).

The track runs diagonally right to the A.64 embankment. Go to the wooden fence ahead and turn left, all the way to the bank of the River Ouse.

Turn sharp right along the bank (S.P. public footpath, Landing Lane).
Pass underneath the A.64 (pictured) and keeping to the riverside path, go through a wooden squeeze gate next to a horse pass, around the left hand curve of the river.
Pass the first building on the right, which is Fulford Hall.

Fulford Hall, up to the right, dates from the early to mid 18th century, although it is reputed to have 11th century origins.
Dates on lead rain buckets around its base range between 1691 and 1745.
A date on the drainpipe top reads 1764.
There are heraldic designs relating to the Keys family on its portals.
It is Grade II listed today.

Simply keep to the riverside footpath all the way round and close to the curve of the river.

Pass through another wooden squeeze gate, next to a horse pass, to reach a picnic area. Observe the notice board about the *exceptionally rare and endangered Tansy Beetle*.

York City Centre lies ahead. What can be said about the historic City of York?
There are so many guide books about this fabulous city.
All of them have much more space and detail than can be afforded here.
Viking, Roman and Medieval remains are amongst the finest in Europe.
Suffice it to say that there is a wealth of history to discover, numerous museums and ancient buildings to explore and modern attractions to visit.

Go over the footbridge in the dip and turn sharp right (S.P. public footpath, Fulford Main Street, Millennium Way) over a small stream at Fulford Ings, and away from the River Ouse.

The Millennium Way is a 24 mile circular walk, starting and finishing at Lendal Bridge in York City Centre.
The route links historic strays and open green spaces around the city of York.

Follow the footpath next to the stream, and then straight ahead on the path past gardens and houses (S.P. public footpath, Minster Way) to reach the main road ahead via Halfpenny Row.

The Minster Way, is a 50 mile walk between the Minsters of Beverley and York, and was established in 1980. It traverses the dry, green valleys of the Yorkshire Wolds before dropping into the Vale of York.

This is Main Street in the Fulford area of York.

Fulford takes it's name from a 'foul' crossing point over either Germany Beck or the River Ouse.
Fulford was the site of a battle on 20th September 1066, when the invasion force of King Harald Hardrada of Norway and his allies defeated forces sent from York.
This was the precursor to the decisive Battle of Stamford Bridge, some five days afterwards, more of which, later.
A tapestry depicting the battle at Fulford is on display in the Merchant Adventurers Hall in York City Centre, having been presented with it by the lady embroiderers of the village in 2011. It took more than five years to complete.
Fulford is the home of the British Army's 15th Infantry Brigade at Imphal Barracks.
The barracks date back to 1795.
It is also the headquarters for the British Military Police.

Fulford to Kexby (9.2 miles, 14.8 km)

Turn right along the main road and cross where it is safe to do so, at the central traffic island lower down the road.

Here, we are on the Minster Way, albeit against the usual direction for this walk.

In a hundred metres or so, turn left down Fordlands Road (S.P. Fulford Cemetery). IGNORE the path to the immediate left (S.P. public footpath, Millennium Way) at this junction.

Cross over the red-brick bridge over Germany Beck on this road, then through a housing estate to the very end of Fordlands Road.

Go straight ahead on a track (S.P. public bridleway. Forest Lane), soon to pass Poplar House Farm on the right.

The track swings to the left, up and over the A.64 by a bridge.

Continue along this track between the fields beyond.

IGNORE the first track to the left and continue straight on to pass a metal gate, just before the building on the left, which is White House Farm.

Go to the left of wooden gates (way-marked Minster Way) and to the left of the barn, into woodland. Continue in a straight line and IGNORE the track as it veers off to the right at the end of the wood.

The path crosses a field, heading for the wooden fence in the trees at the other side. Pass over the water-course by the fence (way-marked Minster Way) and go straight on through the gate to walk alongside the A.64 carriageway at the field edge.

Pass to the left of the electricity pylon, IGNORING the track to the right. Keep alongside the A.64 on the track.

Cross the water-course by the concrete bridge and turn right (S.P. public footpath. Heslington Tillmire).

Walk alongside Heslington Common with the water-course to your right.

Heslington Common, as its name implies, was originally unenclosed pasture founded under the manorial system, for the use of residents. It is now a golf course.

BEWARE of flying golf balls and always give way to golfers.

At the southern edge of the Common, the path turns left (S.P. public bridleway and way-marked Minster Way) by the metal gate and wooden fencing, to pass through trees alongside the golf course.

Heslington Tillmire, to your right, is an area of marsh and fen which is a Site of Special Scientific Interest (SSSI). It is one of the most crucial areas in the Vale of York for ground-nesting birds such as Redshank, Lapwing and Snipe. Numerous other bird species have been sighted here.

Just before you reach open fields, the path turns to the right (S.P. public bridleway, Langwith Stray and way-marked, Minster Way). Go through the metal gate.

Follow this path alongside the hedge-line. IGNORE the first metal gate and track to farm buildings on the left and carry straight on.

Also IGNORE the second and third metal gates on the left.

A water-course dyke joins from the left and the path bears slightly to the right alongside it.

Cross over the dyke by means of a wide, rubber decked wooden footbridge with two metal gates (blue and yellow way-marker).

Once over the dyke, turn right (way-marked Minster Way) and in 150 metres, turn left alongside a branch of the dyke, just before Fir Tree Farm.

Join the tarmac lane, Langwith Stray (way-marked Minster Way) and go straight ahead.

Follow the lane, past Gill Wood and Langwith Lakes fishing ponds on the right.

Langwith Lakes coarse fishery was created in 2003 and extended in 2006, to provide four fishing lakes, over eighteen acres. The lakes are up to four and a half feet deep and anglers can look forward to landing Mirror, Common and Ghost Carp as well as Tench and Barbel. Day tickets are available and regular competitive fishing matches are held here.

Where the road turns sharply to the left, carry straight on along a tarmac track. IGNORE the public bridleway sign over the bridge to the right, and go straight on (S.P. public footpath, Minster Way), onto a green lane, with a water-course on your right.

Pass White House Farm to the left.

Soon afterwards, the path bears slowly to the right, alongside a watercourse on your right and Grimston Wood on your left. Continue along this green lane.

As the wood ends, after the metal gate, turn left (S.P. Minster Way, Kexby) and walk on the right side of the watercourse down a tree lined track, to the left of the electricity poles.

Pass Grange Farm on your left.

This track ends at a T junction with a tarmac road, the B.1228. Turn right here (way-marked Minster Way), along the verge, passing Gipsey Wood Farm on your right.

Elvington airfield, just over to your right, was originally a grass strip, but three hardened runways were built in late 1941, together with accommodation for 2,800 staff. In 1942, it became the base for Bomber Command and housed Halifax bombers. It was also home to the Free French Air Force.

Eighty Halifax aircraft were lost from here in the Second World War, together with over 500 crew either killed, missing in action or taken prisoner.

After the war, it was re-built by the United States Air Force as a base for B47 nuclear bombers. A runway over 10,000 ft. long was constructed. It is one of the longest in the U.K.

The Americans left in 1958, and for several years afterwards, it was used as a test runway for R.A.F. Buccaneer aircraft.

It was designated as an emergency runway for Concorde and as a possible landing site for the U.S. Space Shuttle.

It is now used for air displays, track days and many other events.

On 21st September 2006, Richard Hammond, of the B.B.C. 'Top Gear' programme, was lucky to escape with his life when the jet-powered dragster he was driving crashed at up to 300m.p.h. (480k.p.h) here. He has since fully recovered.

The site also contains the Yorkshire Air Museum, which is open to visitors.

Stay on the right side verge until forced to cross the road (with care) at the wooden fence. Now stay on the left side verge.

50 metres after the wooden fence, take the tarmac lane to the left (White Fox S.P. Kexby Stray).

Pass The Nook, which is a house on your right and continue along the tarmac lane.

Just before a small orchard and large green barn, turn left (way-marked Minster Way), along a dirt track.

Follow this track in a straight line past a large area of woodland on the left, known as Rabbit Warren.

The track runs alongside the wood and then enters a small section of this wood (way-marked Minster Way), carry straight on and over a dismantled railway line (S.P. public bridleway, Minster Way).

Go through the wooden gate opposite (way-marked Minster Way) to Pass White Carr Farm on your right. The path becomes a track and continues all the way to the A.1079.

Cross the road here and go straight across, passing Scoreby Lodge which is just to your left. IGNORE the Private Road sign.

Simply follow this tarmac lane until it turns left, next to a metal gate on the right. At this point, leave the tarmac lane to go straight ahead on a dirt track (S.P. public bridleway, Kexby, and way-marked Minster Way).

Follow this well defined track into Millfield Wood, travel straight through the middle of it.

As you enter Millfield Wood, a track runs immediately off to the right. A windmill once stood at the end of the track in the middle- ages, giving its name to Mill Field. The windmill stood on a mound, which is still visible.

As you emerge from this wood, go straight on to walk alongside further woodland to your left and with a hedge-line to your right.

As the wood ends, go straight on and in 50 metres, the path turns sharp right (way-marked Minster Way, Jorvik Way), across the field and all the way back to the A.1079 at Kexby.

*The Jorvik or Jorvic Way, was created by the Yorkshire Footpath Trust.
It is a 65 mile (104km) circular walk from Tadcaster and takes in villages around the Greater York area, as well as passing the site of the battle of Marston Moor.*

(For those staying at York Rose B & B, turn right where the path joins the A.1079, it is 300 metres on the right.)

*Kexby was originally a Scandinavian settlement.
A toll ferry at the river crossing is first mentioned in historical records in 1315 and finally in 1650.
The first stone bridge is recorded in 1420, and by 1540, was said to have three arches. It was restructured in 1650 and is visible to the right of the new bridge.
The new bridge was built in 1960, which bypassed the old bridge altogether (pictured).
In 1354, Kexby was hard hit by the Black Death plague and tax receipts show a 60% drop in that year.
The area was once heavily wooded and records show that 116 oaks were sold here in 1441, for building work at York Minster.*

Kexby to Stamford Bridge (3.2 miles, 5.4 km)

Turn left along the A.1079 (way-marked Minster Way, Jorvik Way) passing the Riverside Care Complex on your left.

In 100 metres, by the crash barriers and just before the River Derwent, IGNORE the path to the left (S.P. public footpath, Minster Way) and continue along the footpath at the roadside, over the River Derwent.

The River Derwent is around 72 miles in length, rising on Fylingdales Moor in the North York Moors National Park.
It traverses the Vale of Pickering, through Kirkham and joins the River Ouse at Barmby on the Marsh, near Selby. It is navigable for much of its length.

Continue along this roadside footpath for around 500 metres, passing the entrance to Kexby House on the left.

Kexby House is an 18th century Georgian farm-house, retaining many original features and is set in 13 acres.
It has bed and breakfast accommodation and a holiday cottage.

In 25 metres, turn left along the bridleway (S.P. public bridleway, blue and yellow way-marker), go through the gate and across the field towards the left side of barns.

Go through a second gate by a large tree, and continue straight ahead along the left side of the hedge-line.

Soldier's Camp, seen 90 degrees to your left, across the river and in the field to the right of the dyke, is supposedly the place where King Harald Hardrada's men stayed prior to epic battles at Fulford and Stamford Bridge in the 11th century.
Little else is known about the site.

Pass the barns on your right and follow this straight path, going through the gate (way-marked bridleway, blue and yellow way-marker). The path bears very slightly to the left alongside the tree-line and then the hedge-line.

This path soon becomes a wide track through crop fields.

On the bank top to your left, at the far side of the river, Scoreby Manor House can be seen.
The first mention of this building is in 1368, but the present Manor bears a carved date of 1723.
Between this house and the river, once stood the hamlet of Scoreby, now long gone. From records, 14 taxpayers were shown to live here in 1301, and mention is made of a windmill in this area in 1339.
It is not known why the hamlet disappeared, but it may simply have reverted to pasture by the early 1600s, as people moved on to other villages or to burgeoning York.
The hamlet may also have suffered from the after effects of the Black Plague.
Earthworks may still be seen in the fields here, whilst foundations and pottery were unearthed in the 1900's.

Continue straight ahead and just to the right of farm buildings (Town End Farm).

This track joins a tarmac lane, Broad Lane.
Go straight ahead, passing The Granary, The Stables and Town End farm on your left.

Continue along the lane and pass private houses to your right and West Farm on your left, into the village of Low Catton.

Low Catton consists mainly of 18th and 19th century houses and the surrounding farms largely post-date the widespread land enclosures of 1766.
An alehouse was licensed in the late 18th century and the Gold Cup Inn was first mentioned by name in 1851.
To the south of the village is a small area known as the Land of Nod, where five single storey poor houses once stood in the 1830s. Only one remains.
The Land of Nod does not refer to sleep, but means 'wandering'.
In the bible, Cain went to the Land of Nod after murdering his brother, Abel.

(For those staying at Corner Farm, it is one of the last buildings on the right before the lane bends sharply to the right).

The lane bears sharply right at the edge of the village. DO NOT go right with the road here. Pass in front of the Old Rectory on your left.

All Saints church, to the left at the end of Low Catton, dates from the 13th century, and the bell tower, complete with three bells, was added almost a century later.
The tower was rebuilt in the 15th century, but by 1676, the church was in ruin.
A restoration programme saw it rebuilt in the 1860s.
The east window is by the famous 19th century designer, William Morris.
A Manor House, complete with deer park, once stood adjacent to the church and also dates to the 13th century.
It was owned by the Percy family, who were the Lords of the Manor.
The family retained ownership until 1577, and the property lay in ruin forty years later.
The Old Rectory was once the courthouse for the Manor and in the 1470s the villages of High and Low Catton each had their own constable.
The retro streetlamps were erected to celebrate the Jubilee of Queen Elizabeth II.

Take the footpath straight ahead, just after the small triangle of grass, and by the Church Lane road-sign, through the wooden squeeze gate (S.P. Stamford Bridge).

Go down the fenced path and pass the pond on your right.

Go through the squeeze gate at the end of the path and continue in the same line down the tree-lined path, through the wooden gate next to a metal gate.

This path travels to the left side of woodland.

Beck Mill once stood in Smackdown Close on Mill Sike Beck and was first recorded in 1474. This was a water-mill where the process of fulling took place.

Fulling, walking or tucking, was originally the process by which cloth, and particularly woollen cloth, was cleansed of oils and dirt by trampling with bare feet. Human urine was often used as the cleansing agent.
Later processes used water and the cloth was beaten with wooden clubs.
The next process was to stretch and dry the cloth on wooden frames called tenters, suspended there from tenterhooks.
It is from this process that we get the expression being on tenterhooks – held in suspense.
The mill was demolished in 1605.

Follow the footpath into woodland, still on the path, which soon passes open fields to your right. Cross an often dry stream by way of the wooden footbridge.

Turn to the right and then left with the path to then travel through a wooden squeeze gate and a metal gate to re-join the River Derwent.

Keep your eyes peeled for a flash of electric blue along the river here as this stretch is home to resident Kingfishers. They nest in cavities in the river bank and feed on small fish and insects. They are on the amber list of endangered species and there are between five and eight thousand breeding pairs in the U.K.

Go through a further wooden squeeze gate and across a wooden footbridge, and pass under the arched railway bridge (pictured) via the footpath at the field and river edge.

Continue straight ahead on this path then via a wooden squeeze gate, the path goes to the right of the arched stone bridge and emerges into a car park in Stamford Bridge.

Cross the A.166 (yet another Roman road) at the pedestrian controlled traffic lights opposite the Swordsman Public House and turn right.

Earl Tostig, the traitorous brother of the nominated English King Harold, encouraged King Harald Hardrada of Norway to lead a 10,000 strong invasion against his brother.
The fleet landed via the River Ouse at Riccall nr. Selby and routed an English force sent from York, at Fulford.

*King Harold marched 3000 men 180 miles in 4 days, from the south.
(It makes the White Rose Way seem like a short stroll!).
His army defeated the Norsemen in a bloody battle on 25th September 1066 at
Stamford Bridge.
A lone Norseman held Harold's army at bay for some time by standing on the
wooden bridge and fighting fiercely. He was killed when one of Harold's men
floated in a tub under the bridge and thrust a spear upwards through the slats.
The pub sign of the Swordsman Inn depicts this event and the pub contains more
information about the battle on wall plaques.
The area where the battle took place is disputed. Some accounts place it 400 metres
north of the current river bridge, whilst others place it at the old river crossing to
the south at Low Catton.
Harold's army forced the invaders to retreat back to Riccall, where only 24 ships of
the original invasion fleet of 300 escaped.
This was the last Viking battle on English soil.
News then came of a French invasion in Sussex, led by Duke William of Normandy.
Harold marched his troops back to the south coast, where, depleted and exhausted,
they were defeated at the Battle of Hastings on 14th October 1066.
Harold sustained an arrow through the eye and was later brutally killed.
William became known as William the Conqueror and England was ruled by the
Normans from that point.
When the Normans reached this area they named it Pons Belli – Battle Bridge.*

Stamford Bridge marks the halfway point of the White Rose Way.

Stamford Bridge to Malton (16.3 miles, 25.9 km)

We leave the Minster Way at this point.

From the Swordsman Inn, continue to your right, alongside the road through the centre of the village, past the shops, bearing right with the main road to the Battle Monument (pictured) with a standing stone and plaque on the left. This is opposite the Bay Horse Inn.

The large building to the left of the Battle Monument, by the river, is the old corn-mill. There has been such a mill on this site since 1130 and parts of the current building date back to 1591.
The mill was greatly expanded in 1847, with an additional 7 grinding stones and 2 water wheels, showing its size and importance to the area.
In 1964, the mill closed and later became the Cornmill Public House, which itself was converted into the luxury flats you see today.

Take the footpath immediately to the left of the battle monument (S.P. public footpath), through a metal gate to pass the corn-mill flats. Go through the squeeze gate (way-marked public footpath) at the back of the car park to the rear of the flats, and along a walled path by the riverside.

Continue through a wooden gate to walk along the riverside path, through a squeeze gate and then a wooden gate (way-marked public footpath), along the bottom of private gardens. Keep to the riverside path.

Go through another wooden gate and follow the curves of the river.

Pass through three wooden gates in the vicinity of Bleach Farm, which is up to your right on the bank top.

Enter a small wood – you may need to brush aside Himalayan Balsam here, which is rampant in the height of summer.

Himalayan Balsam (or Policeman's Helmet) is a foreign invader and as the name suggests, originates in the Himalayan mountain range of India.
The plant was introduced to the U.K. by the Victorians as an unusual garden plant. It has spread uncontrollably since then and is common throughout England and Wales. It grows up to 6ft 6 inches (2 metres), having green hollow stems which turn red and has distinctive 'gaping mouth' twin pink petals. It is regarded as a nuisance weed now. The ripe seeds pods, when touched, explode and shoot seeds for up to 23 feet (7 metres) with some force, as I found out to my cost. Ouch!

Go through a wooden gate at the end of the small wood and carry straight on through a series of wooden gates, all the time keeping to the riverside through the paddocks.

The path becomes a track alongside the river.

Follow this track as it travels over Barlem Beck by a footbridge. (At the time of printing, this footbridge is missing and will be replaced as soon as possible). This is usually an easy scramble if still missing.

There follows a series of wooden gates and a metal gate along the riverside path as you pass Bank House, which is up to the right.

Just after Bank House, the path enters a small wood alongside the river.

The small green stemmed plant with a cluster of bright red berries often seen here in Summer is Cuckoo Pint, also called Lords and Ladies or Wild Arum.
The berries which are present from July to September are poisonous.

Go through a squeeze gate (way-marked green and yellow arrow) in the woodland.

Go over a small wooden footbridge, taking care on the muddy, banked path ahead.

Exit the wood via a wooden gate, keeping to the riverside.

This path joins a tarmac road via a gate on the right as the river swings to the left.

Turn left along this road for around 100 metres to the T-junction.

Turn left (Road Sign - Buttercrambe, Scrayingham) for 30 metres before turning right into another road (Road Sign – Scrayingham).

Aldby Park, the house seen down to the left, was the birthplace of Thomas Darley in 1664. He became Queen Anne's Consul to Syria and whilst there, he bought an Arabian stallion from Sheik Mirza. The horse was imported to England and although never raced, it was put to stud, until its death at the age of 30 years. The horse became famous as the 'Darley Arabian' and it's great, great grandson was the never beaten 'Eclipse'. It is said that the Darley Arabian's bloodline is contained in 80 - 90% of all race-horses in Britain today.

Walk towards the village of Scrayingham and IGNORE the first road on the right, go through the village and bear right with the road by the church, as it exits the village.

The church of St .Peter and Paul at Scrayingham was built in 1208. It has some 14th century features and was extensively remodelled in 1853.
A south aisle was added to cater for the people of the nearby village of Howsham. The path between the villages, via Plaster Pitts Farm, was known as the coffin road for obvious reasons. By 1860, Howsham had its own church, however.
The grave which contains the most prominent resident is that of George Hudson (d.1871). He became known as the 'King of the Railways' and created many railways throughout the country in his lifetime.
A former Lord Mayor of York, Hudson became involved in financial scandals which led to his trial and imprisonment, after which, his many business interests folded. He died in disgrace.

Pass the church on your left and after the adjacent lone building on the left, take the track to the left immediately after the metal railings and through a wooden gate (S.P. public footpath, way-marked green and yellow arrow). Go left down to the rear of the church (NOTE – some maps show the path in front of the lone building and the church – this is not the case).

At the end of the graveyard, bear 45 degrees right down the hill – DO NOT go over the farm bridge, go to the riverside to the left of this and cross the footbridge (way-marked public footpath), over Swallowpits Beck to walk alongside the River Derwent once more.

Go through a wooden squeeze gate, still alongside the river – more Balsam beating!

The path traverses another beck via a wooden footbridge and a stile.

The trees to your right are young willow trees (if not harvested) and are planted as a crop. They are turned into wood pellets for use in biomass power stations.

The path then enters The Rush, which is a small wood, via another stile on your left.

Cross Whitecarr Beck inside the wood, via the steps and the wooden footbridge.

Turn to the left following the yellow and white way-marker along the riverside footpath which goes gently uphill at first, by the side of a crop field.

The path continues to cling to the riverbank top at the field edge, heading for an electricity pylon ahead.

At the end of this field, cross the wooden footbridge in the dip and pass to the left of the electricity pylon.

Go through the squeeze gate just after the pylon (way-marked public footpath, green and yellow arrow).

Go through the wooden gate (way-marked public footpath, yellow and white arrow), to pass open fields and Paradise Farm on your right.

Pass through a wooden squeeze gate next to a metal gate (way-marked green and yellow arrow). Follow the curve of the river and then over a single gated wooden footbridge (green and yellow way-marker). Continue along the riverside path.

The path goes into riverside woodland via a wooden squeeze gate (way-marked public footpath), before reaching the road at Howsham Bridge (pictured).

Gain the road by the squeeze stile next to the larger gates.

Turn left to cross the bridge at this point.

Turn right immediately after the bridge (S.P. Kirkham), along a footpath which now follows the left side riverbank.

Go through the wooden gate (way-marked green and yellow arrow), into woodland.

Howsham Mill, to the right, was built as a water-powered flour mill around 1755. It is now a Grade II listed building.
The mill closed in 1947 and fell into a state of disrepair over the following decades. In 2004, the Renewable Heritage Trust was formed to raise funds for restoration. The first phase was completed in 2007 with a new waterwheel and an Archimedes screw hydro-electric generator situated next to the weir.
Further building works have since taken place, to renew walls and it is proposed to create an environmental study centre.

At the weir side, go up the steps to the left, cross the footbridge and up more steps to walk along the bank top path.

Cross the next wooden footbridge and go left along the riverside path.

Go through the wooden gate (way-marked green and yellow arrow).

Howsham Hall, on the right riverbank, was a stately home, built in the 17th century and is a Grade I listed building.
It was constructed using stone and timbers from Kirkham Priory, after its fall into ruin. This was held to be sacrilege and it is said that a curse was placed on the house. The Curse of Kirkham states that 'all male heirs of the estate would perish and true happiness would never come to that family or its successors'.
Spookily, this curse has held true in respect of male heirs of the various families who have owned the property to date.
In 1956, it was purchased and converted into an independent boy's school. It later became a mixed school, but closed in 2007, due to lack of numbers. It is a private dwelling today.

IGNORE the path and gate in the fence on your left, keep to the riverside path.

Pass successively through a wooden gate, over two wooden footbridges, a small section of board-walk and a further wooden footbridge which are all way-marked.

Here, you are amongst the Howardian Hills, an Area of Outstanding Natural Beauty (A.O.N.B) and which was granted the status in 1987.
It covers 79 square miles of rolling hills, woods and farmland between Helmsley, Coxwold, Kirkham and the River Derwent.

100 metres after the wooden footbridge, and before the line of trees ahead, NOTE a small way-marked post (sometimes not visible due to overgrowth). The path goes to the right down a distinct path closer to the river. DO NOT continue up the slope of the field.

Another two short stretches of boardwalk are encountered. Keep to the riverside path at the edge of the field.

Pass over a further three way-marked wooden footbridges, still on the riverside path.

The path sticks to the riverbank all the way to Kirkham, passing up into woodland, alongside the railway line, and then a weir to the right.

Pass through a wooden gate at the top side of the weir (green and yellow way-marker). Go straight ahead.

Kirkham Priory to the right, was commenced in 1122, as an Augustinian house, on the site of an earlier church. Major and additional works continued into the 15th century.
In 1539, the Dissolution of the Monasteries saw the Priory stripped and it was sold on in the following year. It began to fall into disrepair and eventually into a ruin.
In the 1920s, pleasure craft were a public attraction on the river at Kirkham.
During World War II, this area was used as a testing and training site for military wading vehicles, which were to be used in the Normandy landings.
Secret visits were made by Winston Churchill and King George VI, to see progress for themselves.

150 metres after passing the weir, gain the road by a wooden squeeze stile and turn right (S.P. Centenary Way) to cross the arched stone bridge to the other side of the river.

The Centenary Way was created to celebrate the 100th year of Yorkshire County Council. It was opened in 1989, by Olympic athlete and pioneer of orienteering in the U.K., Chris Brasher.
The walk is 83 miles long, and follows a meandering route from York to Filey taking in the Howardian Hills, Castle Howard and the deserted medieval village of Wharram Percy.

Follow this road uphill past the remains of Kirkham Priory on the right. (The café here is open at certain times).

As the glaciers retreated in the last ice-age, a glacier still blocked the paths of rivers and streams flowing from the North York Moors into the North Sea.
A huge lake formed in the Vale of Pickering as a result.
As the lake became deeper and wider, it breached its lowest point at Kirkham and water flowed down the valley, scouring away the sides, thus forming the present gorge.

Continue up the hill and just before the Stone Trough Pub, take the road to the left (Road Sign, Firby, Malton), quite steeply uphill, leaving the village behind you. (C'mon, this is the only hill on the whole walk!)

In the 12th century, Walter L'Espec, a French knight, commanded this area.
He oversaw the King's rights in this region, in the reign of Henry I of England.
He was the founder of Kirkham Priory and later Rievaulx Abbey, going on to build castles at Helmsley and at Wark in Northumbria.
Walter led the Yorkshire barons against King David I of Scotland and his army at the Battle of the Standard, near Northallerton in 1138, after which the Scots were forced to retreat as far north as Carlisle.
Walter died in 1153 and is buried at Rievaulx. Commemorative windows to him and his son can be found at All Saints Church in Helmsley.
Walter's young son was killed in a riding accident near Kirkham, and to commemorate him, Walter erected a stone cross on a base.
Whilst the stone cross has long since disappeared, the base may be seen at the entrance to the car park of the pub. The hollow in the base where the cross stood, was often mistaken for a trough, hence the name Stone Trough Cottage.
The public house was opened in 1983, when the cottage was restored.

As the road levels out, IGNORE the first footpath on the left (S.P. Firby), as this footpath was officially deleted in January 2011. It will be present on maps for some time and bear in mind that the fingerpost will be removed at some stage.

Continue along this road and take the first road on the left (Road Sign, Firby Only) and into the village of Firby.

Pass Firby Hall, which is on your left.

Firby Hall, is a Grade II listed building, and was built in the Georgian period. Schoolchildren from Hull were evacuated and billeted here during World War II, to escape the numerous bombing raids on their home city.

The children attended local schools and worked on the land at local farms, vital tasks in the war effort.
It is now split into wings to form private dwelling houses and still has the original walled gardens and stables.

Turn first right down a tarmac lane (S.P. River Derwent), and this soon becomes a track.

Pass the last farmhouse on the left and go straight ahead down the track towards woodland, which is Coldwell Plantation. Go through the gap in the trees ahead, on the track.

The path then bears left after Coldwell Plantation, by the field-side, with trees to your left. Follow the field-side path to the left corner of the field and go down the path to the left into woodland at the clearly sited white post.

Head downhill, to pass through a wooden gate (green and yellow way-marker), exit the wood and then cross a small pasture to reach the riverside again.

Turn right alongside the river and to the right of riverbank trees.

The Blackthorn bushes to your left produce a prodigious amount of sloes.
These are dusty looking, stoned black fruit when ripe, slightly smaller than grapes. They are green in the ripening process.
They are ready to pick in September/October and are used in jams, sloe gin, sloe brandy and even sloe vodka. These would be ready to drink at Christmas. Cheers!

Continuing to follow the riverside path, go through a wooden gate (green and yellow way-marker), followed by two short stretches of boardwalk to then cross a stream by a single gated wooden footbridge.

Enter Jeffry Bog Plantation Nature Reserve (sign on gate). Go straight ahead.

The path crosses a stream by a wooden footbridge.

As you leave this Plantation via a single gated wooden footbridge, you will see a **notice board about the Plantation**, just to your right. Turn right here, away from the river and all the way up the right hand side of the field.

Go through a gate (green and yellow way-marker) at the top right end of the field and up a short track to join the road, opposite the entrance to Church Farm Kennels.

Turn left along the road for a couple of hundred metres and take the first road on the left (S.P. Centenary Way, Road Sign - Menethorpe).

The road goes downhill over a stream, then uphill and travels between the river on your left and a stretch of woodland on your right.

Keep your ears and eyes open for the screeching calls of common buzzards which nest in these woods. They can often be seen soaring and gliding on the thermals. They are brown with a rounded tail and have white flashes at the underside wing tips.

When the road turns sharp right, take a tarmac path (S.P. Centenary Way) to the left next to a small lay-by.

Cross a stream by a small metal railed bridge.

DO NOT cross the river via the large metal suspension bridge on your left.

Go straight ahead through the wooden squeeze gate (S.P. public footpath) and keep to the right hand side of the river.

This path travels under the railway bridge (S.P. Centenary Way) and follows the right hand riverbank all the way into Malton.

Simply pass through several way-marked gates, stiles and a small wooden footbridge, all the while keeping to the riverside footpath.

On nearing Malton, the path runs between the river and the railway line, passing beneath electricity cables. The path continues by the riverside.

Go through the wooden gate (way-marked public footpath) and along the grassy path beyond.

Go through the floodgate in the red-brick wall to pass a playground near to houses. This short road emerges opposite the Bus and Railway Stations, in Railway Street on the boundary of Norton and Malton.

Turn left on Railway Street. At the T junction at the top of the street, turn right along the A.1257, Yorkersgate, and first left at the traffic lights into Wheelgate.
This is the main shopping street.

The town of Malton was initially settled by the Romans around AD71, as Derventio, and their fort stood where the town centre is today. Ruins may still be seen.
The fort was vacated in AD 429, near to the end of the Roman Empire.
In 1138, the Archbishop of York ordered the town to be burned, to rid it of Scots, who had occupied it. The re-building work led to the creation of New Malton, making it distinct from Old Malton.
The town has a Charles Dickens connection, in that Dickens wrote his famous novel, 'A Christmas Carol', whilst staying here with a friend.
There is a long brewing history here and at one time, nine breweries plied their trade. Sadly, the last one, Suddaby's, contracted brewing work out of the town in 2010 when 'treated' water became the main supply in Malton, which badly affected the taste and finish of the brewed products.
Their beers are now made by Leeds Brewery and the Brown Cow Brewery at Selby. Malton also has a long history connected with horseracing.
There are several famous stables and stud farms in the area, many of which have open days.

This road becomes Newbiggin after Princess Road on the right.
Continue straight ahead, up Newbiggin.

Malton to Thornton Le Dale (10.2 miles, 16.4 km)

At the next major junction, which is traffic-light controlled, turn right into Pasture Lane and then in 25 metres, turn left into Outgang Road.

This is a tarmac country lane (S.P. public bridleway), which becomes a dirt track after the allotments on the left.

Continue along this track to pass over the A.64 as it becomes a tarmac lane again.

IGNORE the first public footpath to the left and Lowfield Road on the right, which is a stony track after the house, and continue straight ahead on the stony lane (green box sign – public bridleway). **Note** that none of the lanes ahead have road name signs.

At the point where the track forks, take the right hand fork along the field end into Ryton Style Road, which is also a stony lane, with a dyke to your immediate left.

IGNORE a track on the left and go straight ahead, to the right of woodland. Continue to the T junction of lanes, with Eden Camp ahead of you, just to the right, and to the left of power lines.

Eden Camp is a Modern History Theme Museum. In 1942, the land was requisitioned by the War Office and a temporary Prisoner of War Camp was built. It soon took in 250 Italians, who were tasked with making a more permanent establishment. At the end of 1943, the Italians made way for Polish soldiers who used the camp as billets prior to the invasion of Europe.
From 1944 to 1949, it reverted to a Prisoner of War Camp, this time for Germans. In the 1950s, the units were subsequently let to local businesses as workshops. It was later turned into a war themed museum, opening in 1987.
It has been constantly enlarged and updated and is now a popular tourist and educational attraction.

Turn left at this T junction into Borough Mill Lane, another stony lane.
Go past the red and white metal barrier.
IGNORE the track to the right in 25 metres.

Pass a concrete silage area and wooden shed on your left in a further 150 metres.

25 metres past the shed, turn right down Great Sike Road, also a stony lane (S.P. arrow symbol, on the left).

IGNORE a track to the left 25 metres before Windmill Farm and continue straight ahead, passing the farm on your right

Originally known as Old Malton Mill, this former flour mill is more than 200 years old. It had a relatively short working life however, as the wind-sails were blown off and destroyed during a violent storm in 1906. The mill was never re-opened as a working mill, although it is now maintained and used for storage.

Continue straight ahead to reach a T junction. Turn left here, along Eden House Road, which is a tarmac lane.

Pass Eden House on your right, Eden Farm on your left and Mews Cottage on your right.

IGNORE the public bridleway to the right through the trees, and continue straight ahead, crossing the River Rye at Ryton Bridge.

The River Rye commences at the foot of the Cleveland Hills, east of Osmotherly, and runs through Hawnby, Rievaulx, Helmsley and other smaller villages before joining the River Derwent near Malton.
The new road bridge here is a recent construction and incorporates wide earth bank flood barriers, allowing the river in spate to create a flood plain.
Over to the right, sand martins can be seen nesting in the mud banks of the river in Spring and Summer. These birds migrate to spend the winter in South Africa.

200 metres past the river embankment, on the far side of the river, take the footpath on your right (green box sign – public footpath), just before Rye Farm.

Cross the stile into a field at the side of the farm.

Cross the field diagonally to the far right corner and cross the stile to walk with a dyke and hedgerow on your right, at the field side.

As you come to a line of trees at a right angle to you, look straight ahead for a short finger post (S.P. green and yellow arrow), which is 10 metres to the left of an old metal gate. Cross the ditch here in the tree line and go straight ahead into the field and walk to the left of the hedge-line.

Pass Abbotts Farm, which is 50 metres to your left.

As you reach a wooden fence, the path takes a little zig-zag to left and right (green and yellow way-markers) and through a crop field (head to the left of a telegraph pole and the right hand end of woodland at the far side).

Cross Costa Beck by a concrete bridge, through the metal gate.

Follow the track and cross the cattle grid into a lane, turning right here, passing Grove House Farm on your left.

Walk along this lane, passing Grove Lodge on your right to reach the main road, which is the A.169.

Cross the road with care and turn right for 50 metres, just before Howe Bridge Farm (Farm shop and café).

The path goes to the left of the barns and farmhouse, over a stile by the tree-line, (S.P. public footpath – no through route).

Go straight ahead and cross a small ladder stile at the side of the barn, and up a paddock.

Exit the paddock via a gate stile at the top right end (green and yellow way-marker).

Follow the track left and bear left with the track, then right, to walk along the left side of the hedgerow.

The path joins a stony lane on a corner. Turn left here. (The lane to the right leads to a path which has been blocked – hence the earlier warning about a no through route).

Go along this lane to join the main tarmac road at a T – junction. Turn right along the road, which is a quiet country lane.

Pass the entrance to Wath Hall Farm on your right and Sheep Foot Grange on your left.

Follow the road, passing the church on the right and into the hamlet of Low Marishes.

The church of St. Francis is a farmer's church with a highly unusual timber clad spire, which is more reminiscent of the Alps.
The parish celebrated the church's 150th anniversary in 2011.

Pass the former School House Inn, on the left, opposite a telephone box, and continue to follow this long lane as it passes the entrances to White House Farm, Riggs Farm, Viaduct House and Swallow Barn, Holme Farm, Bacon Farm and Selley Bridge Farm.

400 metres or so after Selley Bridge Farm, the road swings sharply to the right and left to cross Thornton Beck via the road bridge.

75 metres past the bridge, turn left down a track towards Newstead Grange.
Go into the farmyard and pass between the barns on your left and the house on your right (yellow way-marker).

Go through the wooden gate (green and yellow way-marker) and bear left to go through the metal gate ahead (yellow way-marker).

Go straight ahead to walk along the track to the right of the hedgerow.

At the power line pole, go straight ahead, continuing along the same line, crossing the crop field on the path.

At the field top, turn right alongside the hedge and dyke for 40 metres and turn left over a two gate wooden bridge. Once over the dyke, go straight ahead along the field side, between the post and wire fence and the hedge.

Cross a single gate wooden bridge and continue straight ahead, again between a post and wire fence and the hedge.

Cross another two gate wooden bridge and continue straight ahead to the left of the hedgerow with an open field to your left.

IGNORE the track to the right with metal gates and continue along the track next to the hedge.
Bear left by a large tree at the field end for 10 metres and cross the stile to your right.

The public footpath crosses the crop field ahead 45 degrees to the left, but the path is sometimes indistinct due to new planting. You may wish to go left around the field edge to reach the same point at the far side if crops are present.

At the other side of the field, bear slightly to the right (old stile on the left), with trees on your left and go up the field.

Thornton Beck is now immediately to your left.

IGNORE the wooden footbridge on the left and carry straight on, to the right of trees, still following the line of the beck.

Keep to the right of the hedge as the beck swings away left, to pass the water treatment works on your left.

Bear left with the track after the works and turn right along the right bank of the beck at the field side (DO NOT cross the beck here). Pass the red and white gas post on your left.

Go over a stile (green and white way-marker), keeping to the beck-side and then left over a gated wooden bridge, crossing the beck, into a paddock.

Head diagonally right across the field, to the right of an electricity pole and cross the stile to gain the road.

At the road, cross over to the other side and turn right to travel into the centre of Thornton Le Dale.

Originally just Thornton, there is evidence of Neolithic and Roman settlement and around A.D.500, the area was invaded and conquered by the Angles.
The village name relates to thorn bushes.
It has a market charter dating back to 1281.
The 'Le Dale' suffix was added after the village received several 'prettiest village' titles in the 1920s and 30s. Still very picturesque, the village is a tourist hot-spot.

Thornton Le Dale to Harwood Dale (15.7 miles, 25.4 km)

At the junction with the A.170, turn right. Cross the road, where it is safe to do so. Pass cafes and a row of single storey stone cottages on your left – **(Lady Lumley's Almshouses – see plaque on wall).**

On reaching Thornton Beck immediately after Bridge Foot Guest House at the road-bridge, turn to the left along the beck-side footpath to pass Beck Isle Cottage on your left.

Beck Isle, a 17th century thatched cottage by Thornton Beck, is reputed to be the most photographed house in the U.K. Go on, take another one!
It has featured on calendars, jig-saws and, in days gone by, on the lids of famous brand chocolate boxes.

Follow this path, all the way to Priestmans Lane. Go over the wooden foot bridge opposite Beck Hall, and turn right along this lane.

Turn left into Church Lane just before reaching the A.170, with the church to your right.

All Saints church is of 14th century origin but is thought to be built on the site of an earlier Anglo Saxon church.
Sir Richard Cholmley (1460 – 1521), also known as the Black Knight of the North, is thought to be buried in the chancel here.
He was appointed a Knight for his services in the battle of Flodden (1513) against the Scots. He was later given the position of Lieutenant of the Tower of London and Supervisory General of 12 Yorkshire castles and manors.
He is the only true historical figure to appear in a Gilbert and Sullivan opera, featuring as the 'Yeoman of the Guard'.

Walk the full length of Church Lane to the T junction with Outgang Lane.

Turn left into this lane with Vale View bungalow on your right and go up the slope. Pass the 'dead end' sign immediately to your right, IGNORING the first lane and green box public footpath sign, to your left, to carry straight on up the slope. It then levels out.

IGNORE the green box public footpath sign on the left after Thornton Dale Service Reservoir to continue straight ahead. Paper Mill Farm is in the valley bottom to your left as the track bears to the right. Keep on this track.

The track varies to a dirt surface.

Welham Park Fish Hatchery, down to the left and slightly behind you, is a fish farm noted for it high quality brown trout. Many fishing clubs purchase the hatchlings to stock rivers and ponds over which they have fishing rights.

IGNORE the green box sign, public bridleway, to the right and keep straight ahead.

The vast expanse of Dalby Forest lies down the slope away to your left. Carry on straight ahead and when the track forks, takes the left fork, continuing up the slope and then around the rim of the valley.

The valley is still down to your left and a disused quarry appears on your right. Keep to the track, with woodland on your left. Continue straight ahead on the same track, (pictured), IGNORING tracks off to the left into the wood.

Keep to the right of woodland on this track, although a few trees do appear on the right of the track as it bends to the right.

Pass through a wooden gate onto a short stretch of footpath. Go straight ahead here, IGNORING the track away to the left at the gate.

In 30 metres, go straight across the main track ahead of you, and go along the footpath straight ahead, flanked by gorse and trees.

The path enters open countryside. Go straight ahead with a few scattered trees to your right and a crop field to your left.

The path soon bends to the right at the end of the scattered trees, to join a track. Turn left on this track, which is Givendale Rigg.

Head for the gap in the trees, straight ahead, passing through the crop fields on either side of you.

This path is now part of The Blue Man Walk, although we will be walking against the intended direction for this walk.
The Blue Man Walk was developed and way-marked by the Forestry Commission. It runs for 16 miles from Reasty Bank Top in the north of the forest, to Allerston in the south. It does not attract many walkers because of the remote start and finish points and there are plans to re-align and revamp the walk.

Enter the gap in the trees (green and yellow way-marker), and continue straight ahead along a stony track.

In Spring and early Summer, there are a profusion of small spiky pink plants in this area in the verges. The petals have fine loops of purple lines. These are Common Spotted Orchids and as the name suggests, they are common throughout the U.K.

Also watch out for many varieties of butterflies, from Small Blues to Dark Green Fritillaries and more common species.

Keep to this long, straight and stony track IGNORING various tracks to left and right.

Continue in a straight line until you come to Givendale Head Farm on your right. Carry on for a short distance, to a T junction of tracks opposite the farm. Go straight ahead (way-marked Moors to Sea Cycle Route).

The Moors to Sea Cycle Route links Pickering, Scarborough, Robin Hood's Bay, Whitby and Great Ayton by means of 107 miles of cycle route, mainly within the North York Moors National Park.
The routes traverse forest, moor and coastline, and have several interlinking stretches and loops for the off-road cyclist.

In 100 metres, take the track to the left (way-marked Moors to Sea Cycle Route), going away from the farm, which is to your right.
This path dips and rises again, and bears to the right, towards the farm (way-marked Moors to Sea Cycle Route).

Pass through a wooden gate to reach a tarmac lane.

Turn right on the lane (way-marked Moors to Sea Cycle Route) to pass the entrance Givendale Head Farm, on your right. Continue along this lane.

IGNORE the first stony track down to the left opposite a car passing place and continue along the lane, passing a low stone wall and metal gate on the right.

In 100 metres, IGNORE the tarmac lane to your left opposite a lay-by (construction site), but 5 metres past this, take the track on the left (S.P. Public Right of Way) parallel to the tarmac lane and now with trees to your immediate right.

Follow this path as it passes pig pens to your left.
In 880 metres, the path passes to the right of forestry, albeit with a few trees to the right too.

IGNORE the track to the right (S.P. public bridleway).

Pass a metal horse gate, still following the same line ahead (way-marked Moors to Sea Cycle Route).

The path soon drops downhill into woodland. Keep straight ahead IGNORING S.P. public footpath, to the right.

Go through a wooden gate and cross the meadow straight ahead, still on the path.

Bear left at a tarmac road (Snainton Lane), and you will come to Cockmoor Hall car park to your right. There is a viewpoint from here down the valley to your left.

Go through the car park to the right, on a stony track, slightly uphill and curving to the left. This becomes a tarmac lane (S.P. Wrench Green and Tabular Hills Walk).

The Tabular Hills Walk commences at Scalby Mills in Scarborough and meanders for 49 miles across the North York Moors via the Hole of Horcum and Cropton, terminating at Helmsley.

Go through the wooden gate next to a metal gate and follow the stony track uphill before it then levels out.
Continue along this track with forestry to your left. It passes into woodland and in just over a mile (1500 metres), the track joins a tarmac road (Cockmoor Road), which comes in from the right.

Go straight ahead along this tarmac road travelling in the same line as the track you have just left, to pass Wykeham Nurseries on your right.

Wykeham Nurseries is operated by the Forestry Commission and produces seeds, plants and trees for re-stocking forestry in the U.K., mainly for timber production. They have a policy of continuous genetic quality improvement by means of pest control and a selection and breeding programme.
Production is largely of pine, spruce, conifer and broad-leaved tree species.
Large cold stores are on site to assist with storage prior to transportation.
Wykeham is one of three such nurseries in the U.K., the others being at Chester and in Scotland. The other two centres produce 20 million trees between them annually.

Continue along the road to pass Brompton Moor House to your left (S.P. Moors to Sea Cycle Route and Tabular Hills Walk).

Continue along this tarmac road, IGNORING all tracks to right and left.

200 metres up the track to the left of the sign 'Raptor Viewpoint', is a viewing area popular with ornithologists and bird-spotters.
Common Buzzards and Honey Buzzards may be seen from here, along with occasional Goshawks and other birds of prey.
The Honey Buzzard is quite rare in the U.K. with up to 70 pairs at any one time. They are summer visitors, from May to September and spend the winter in tropical Africa. They feed on the larvae of wasps and bees and have spectacular brown and white barred plumage on the underside of their wings.

Continue to follow the tarmac road, until it swings very sharply to the right. At this point, there is a small car park on the left.

Turn left at the car park, away from the road, and go down a tarmac footpath to the left (S.P. public footpath, Moors to Sea Cycle Route and Ravenscar).
There are seats, a viewpoint and an **information board** just up to the right here.

Woodland acreage in Britain has been in decline since the middle ages.
It reached a record low as a consequence of the Industrial Revolution, which required huge amounts of timber for railway sleepers and for burgeoning industrial developments.
The supply of wood became particularly acute during the First World War.
The demand for trench linings and pit props for the mines became critical, as imports could not be relied on.

A Committee set up to examine the situation led to the Forestry Act of 1919, which created the Forestry Commission. This body is now responsible for woodland in the U.K. The first trees were planted in Devon and over the years, forestry acreage increased dramatically.
By 1990, multi purpose forestry and conservation became the focus, restoring native trees and opening woodland for leisure purposes.

The tarmac path drops down quite sharply to the left through Highwood Brow, becoming a stony track, and is soon joined by another track coming in uphill from the right.

Bear to the left along the track here (Moor Road). The track soon bears to the left and right.

IGNORE the track off to the left and go straight ahead (S.P. Moors to Sea Cycle Route, green and yellow way-marker), down the hill.

The track becomes tarmac again just on the hairpin bend at the bottom of the hill and then reverts to a stony track once more.

In 75 metres, go straight over the track 'crossroads', and also the next track 'crossroads' (S.P. Moors to Sea Cycle Route).

Pass a metal barrier and soon after this, the track crosses a stream and reaches a road (Estell Lane).

Cross straight over this road and over the wooden stile opposite, to take the footpath into the field (green box sign, public footpath).

Climb the small earth bank immediately to your right and turn left up the field by the tree-line.

Go to the top of the field and turn 90 degrees to the right at an old tree stump and to the right of a line of trees, walking in a small gully.

Go through a wooden gate (green and yellow way-marker, diversion sign) and straight ahead. In 5 metres, turn left up the track (as the path shown going straight ahead on maps has been diverted).

In another 100 metres, at a wooden gate, go to the right of it, NOT through it (green and yellow way-marker, diversion sign) and around the field top with trees to your left.

As the woods to your left come to an end, look for a stile on the left (green and yellow way-marker) at the top end of the single line of trees which go downhill. Go over it and turn 30 degrees to your right, down the field.

Head for the way-marked stile next to a forked tree, situated at the other side of the field.
Cross the stile (green and yellow way-marker) and turn 45 degrees to your left down the hill through bracken and then gorse.
On reaching the tree-line, go 10 metres to the left and over the stile (green and yellow way-marker). Go left alongside a post and wire fence.

Go to the left of a metal gate and to the left of the infant River Derwent.

In 40 metres, turn right over an old stone packhorse bridge over the Derwent and go straight ahead on the path.
Go through the wooden gate ahead (green and yellow way-marker) to the rear of Bridge Farm and gain the road via a second wooden gate.

At the road (Broxa Lane), turn right and cross the River Derwent via the road bridge. At the other side, take the path in 20 metres to your left, going over the stile (green box sign, public footpath).

Time to relax from reading, as the clear path simply follows the River Derwent to your immediate left, for almost four miles along the valley bottom, and only two stiles to climb!

Keep to the obvious riverside path in the valley bottom, IGNORING any paths off to the right. The River Derwent is never far away to the left.

After the second stile and all the way up the valley to the wooden footbridge at Hingles Wood, under the trees in the forest you may notice a series of large mounds of pine needles at the path-side.
Look more closely and you will see that they are actually ant's nests or formicaries. These are home to Northern Wood Ants, which live in colonies up to half a million strong. They build these nests from needles and woodland detritus. The colonies have chambers and pathways extending underground. The nests may be up to a metre in height and several metres in circumference. The ants feed on honeydew, a sugary substance produced by aphids, though they will also feed on invertebrates. Their presence is an indicator of healthy woodland, as they disperse seeds and feed on leaf damaging insects. They are themselves a source of food for some woodland birds. Do not disturb these mounds as the ants are aggressive when attacked and can spray formic acid from their abdomens for up to 12 cm.

Where the river obviously forks, just west of Hingles Wood, follow the bank of the right fork for a short distance and cross the river by the wooden footbridge (S.P. Blue Man symbol).

At the far bank, in 15 metres, turn right along the footpath through Hagg Wood, IGNORING the smaller path off to the left. You are now to the left of Harwood Dale Beck.

Keep to the main beck-side path, the beck is always 10 – 20 metres to your right at most.

You will reach Low North Camp, an old military training ground with concrete tracks and the remains of buildings. Be aware of traffic here.

Low North Camp was created during World War Two as a British Army training camp. This was in use up to the 1960s.
It has been converted into an off-road motor cycle training and trials event area. The Scarborough and District Motor Club organise regional and national trials here. Amazing clips of the skills needed to negotiate the courses can be seen on YouTube.

Go straight ahead on the concrete track.

At a T-junction of concrete tracks, take the track to the right, bear left with it and continue along it going straight ahead, still following the line of the beck.
Go through a green metal gate to reach the road.

Turn right over Lownorth Bridge and the road now has a tarmac surface.
Follow this road to a 'Give Way' T junction and turn right along Reasty Road (no road signage).

The Mill Inn, 600 yards up the road to the left, is a traditional Yorkshire pub as it used to be. It started life in the 1700s as a mill and was later converted into a public house. The same family have run the pub since 1941.
It has no modern refinements and is open seasonally, from April to October.
It is a very popular venue for cyclists and walkers.

The road is level, and then heads uphill. Pass the road signs for 'double bend' and '16% gradient'.

100 metres past these signs take the footpath on the left (green box sign, public footpath).

Go through the right hand metal gate and walk down the field side to the field bottom. Turn right at the wire fence.

In 100 metres, turn left to pass over the beck and through wooden gates.

Go diagonally right across the field towards Hardwick Farm. Pass to the immediate left of the farmhouse and turn left at the far side of the first barn. Turn right up the concrete drive and through wooden gates to reach the road.

Turn right at the road and pass St. Margaret's church on your right.

St. Margaret's church was built in 1862 and is Early English Gothic in style.
It has one bell in the tower. It replaced an earlier St. Margaret's, built in 1634.
The ruins of this earlier church can still be seen further up the village.

Continue through the hamlet of Harwood Dale along this road.

Follow the road as it turns right opposite the drive to Moor Cottage Farm and follow it downhill and then round to the right. 50 metres after the telephone box take the footpath to the right (green box sign, public footpath) and go through the wooden gate.

Cross the grassy yard and exit via a wooden gate at the far side (green and yellow way-marker).

The footpath turns sharply to the left. Follow the path up the open field by the hedge-line and then up to a large wooden gate (green and yellow way-marker).

The Grainery at Keasbeck Hill Farm, for those people staying here, is accessed by going through the small wooden gate to the left of the large gate and up the path to the farm on your left. Return to this large gate the following day.

Harwood Dale to Cloughton (4.2 miles, 6.7 km)

Having gone through (or over) the large gate, continue to follow the hedge-line on the left and around the open field on the right.

Go through the wooden gate at the field end (green and yellow way-marker) and turn sharp right at the edge of the crop field to travel down to the field bottom.

DO NOT GO THROUGH the small wooden gate at the field bottom.

Instead, turn left to go round the field with a hedge to your right. Go through the large gate on the right (green and yellow way-marker).

Go diagonally right to the electricity pole (green and yellow way-marker) and to the stone wall directly beyond it, passing Grange Farm 200 metres to your left.

Climb the stone stile in the wall on your left by the metal gate and go straight ahead by the hedge-line.

You will reach a track. Go left through the metal gate and then immediately sharp right to travel down a tarmac lane.

The stone and turf structure to your immediate right is a lime-kiln. Its presence is the indication of an ancient road. This kiln is one of four in the local area.
Most date from medieval times and were in use up to the 19th century.
Lump limestone, crushed by hand, was loaded into the bowl, interspersed with coal or kindling, and burned to produce quicklime.
A typical process took a day to load, three days to burn and a day to unload.
The workers slept by the kiln at night throughout the process.
The resultant quicklime was used in mortar and limewash, but most importantly as a fertiliser for the land. Local field conditions had high moisture content, but were low in nutrients. Quicklime spread on the land improved the fertility of these acidic soils leading to greater crop productivity and improved grazing.

Turn left through a wooden gate (S.P. Moorend Road and Thirley, green and yellow way-marker) or over the adjacent stile and up the field to the left of Burgate Farm.

Burgate Farm is a family run business which has been developed over the last forty years. There are over 300 dairy cattle as well as a small herd of rare breed pigs. Their 'Oxford Sandy and Black' pigs won the breed championship at the Great Yorkshire Show in 2011. The farm supplies fresh milk to local Morrison's supermarkets.
It is also a bed and breakfast business, specialising in guests bringing their own horses.

Go through a metal gate and straight ahead next to a post and wire fence. At the fence end, turn right up the slope (S.P. Thirley) and climb the wooden ladder stile in the hedge.

Follow this path across fields using the first electricity pole as a marker.

Bear slightly right after the pole (green and yellow way-marker) and go through the electric fence at the gap between two fence posts (green and yellow way-marker).

Cross the track and go through the gap between two fence posts straight ahead of you. Go straight ahead, making for the two trees situated at the field corner.
Cross the stile over the wall (green and yellow way-marker).

Head up the field to the left tree of two trees ahead. Continue straight across the field in the same line to a large wooden gate at the far side of the field (green box sign public footpath).

Go over the stile next to the wooden gate to enter Waite Lane.

The water table in this area is high, leading to the surrounding fields having high water content. The modern name of this lane is Waite Lane, but this is a corruption of its old name Wade Lane, with its obvious meaning.

Go straight over this lane, crossing the stile (green box sign, public footpath) still on the footpath, passing just south of Ellis Close Farmhouse.

Go diagonally left to a metal gate at the far side. Pass just to the right of twin electricity poles to the stile in the fence at the far side. Cross this stile (green and yellow way-marker) and go 45 degrees to your left, aiming for the highest point of the hill ahead of you.

At the hilltop, head for the wall corner, downhill and straight ahead.

Walk close to the left of the wall (green and yellow way-marker post) towards the trees.

Cross a stile, a wooden footbridge and a second wooden stile.

Turn left, to the wall corner under the trees.

Head for the wooden gate, which is just to the left of the barns at Thirley Beck Farm.

Turn left through the gate (S.P. public footpath) and go through a second wooden gate (green and yellow way-marker).

Cross the paddock and go through the metal gate at the top left.

Go right up the track, then through the farmyard to join Harwood Dale Road.

Turn right along the road.

Pass Ellis Close farm on your right and after the road has crossed Brown Beck in the dip, turn left along the footpath (green box sign, public footpath, green and yellow way-marker) just after the pumping station.

Walk up the field keeping close to the hedge-line on your left.

Mid-way along a small stretch of woodland on your left, and at a metal gate (green and yellow way-marker) the path turns sharp right.

DO NOT GO THROUGH THIS METAL GATE. Turn right up the field with the hedge-line to your left.
At the field top go over the stile straight ahead (green and yellow way-marker), and turn immediately right with a wall on your right, for 30 metres.

Turn left at the wall and cross the field edge with the wall on your right.

Climb a stile over a wall to reach Gowland Lane.

Turn right along the lane for 50 metres, and take the track to the left (green box sign, public footpath). It enters woodland via a wooden gate and this wide track soon bears to the left, going uphill.

You will shortly come to a way-marker post on the left.

20 metres after the way-marker post, DO NOT CONTINUE UPHILL ON THE TRACK AHEAD, take the track to the right, downhill through Oxdale Slack.

There is a green and yellow way-marker post on the left, down the hill.
Cross the wooden footbridge and up the hill at the other side. Go through a wooden gate (green and yellow way-marker) and go up the gully, to emerge into fields to the right of Ripley's Farm.

Follow the path with a wall to your right. Go through the metal gate and straight on to reach a tarmac lane (Ripley's Road) via another metal gate, with the drive to the farmhouse to your left.

Go straight across the lane, through a metal gate onto a track with a wall to your left. Go through the next metal gate and go straight ahead just to the left of a line of boulders and gorse.

Enter the track going downhill between the gorse bushes.

Follow the fence and tree-line to a large metal gate. Go through and along the track straight ahead.

Follow the track past the rear of a farm as the track then becomes a tarmac lane.

In 100 metres, take the footpath through woodland to the immediate left of Quarry Close Cottage as the tarmac lane turns to the right.

At the football field, DO NOT walk down the steps to the right, go straight ahead and through a metal gate ahead of you, then along the field bottom with a wall to your right.

200 metres after the football field turn right at the fence corner and through a metal gate. Follow the path uphill into trees and a gully.

Follow the gully round to the right to emerge onto a tarmac lane.

The church over to the right is St. Mary's. The Reverend G.P.Taylor was the vicar here and he went on to become a best selling children's author.
He is an ex police officer (just like me) and self published his first book (just like me), achieving phenomenal sales through word of mouth (just like me?).
His first book Shadowmancer (2002) and subsequent title Wormwood (2004) made him a world travelled multi-millionaire (just like…...well, maybe not).
Come on – tell all your friends about my book!

Go over the ford and take the footpath to the immediate left after it (S.P. public footpath), through a wooden gate.

Go over the wooden footbridge (green and yellow way-marker) and turn right along field edge. Pass a railway sleeper bridge on the right and go to the right of the cricket pitch (pictured) via a squeeze gate.

IGNORE the first footpath exit (green and yellow way-marker) and take the path through the gap in the low wall (next to a wooden post and a white sign re dogs) ahead.

Keep on the paved path to the right of houses to emerge onto the A171.

Turn right along the road into the village of Cloughton.

Cloughton to Scarborough (6.8 miles, 10.9 km)

In the village, where the road turns sharply to the right in 150 metres, take the road to the left which is Newlands Road. Turn IMMEDIATELY right into Newlands Lane. This road leads downhill, then uphill, past Court Green Farm.

Look for the bridge on the sky-line ahead. Turn right just before the bridge, along the footpath. This path joins the track-bed of the old Scarborough to Whitby railway line where you should turn to the right, down the old track-bed.

The 21 mile, Scarborough to Whitby railway line was opened on 16th July 1885, and was built and owned by an independent company.
It opened up the resort of Robin Hood's Bay to holidaymakers for the first time.
The line was expensive to build, due to the engineering problems encountered in tackling the severe gradients and was not profitable. The company ran into debt and the line was sold to the much larger, North Eastern Railway just three years later, in 1888.
The line finally closed on 8th March 1965, as part of what many consider to be the short sighted and ill considered, Dr. Beeching cuts.
The track-bed is now a popular footpath and cycleway called the Scarborough to Whitby Trailway.

On reaching the old Cloughton railway station, go through the wooden gate, cross the road and go left into the yard of the old station (café tea-rooms here now).

Pass the old goods shed on the left to re-join the track-bed via a wooden gate.

Continue for three quarters of a mile (1100 metres) to Field Lane in Burniston, which is the first lane that the track-bed crosses.

Go over the stone railway bridge above this lane and turn immediately right, down the banking steps to the tarmac lane.

Turn right on this lane, under the bridge and uphill towards the coast. Pass bungalows on the left and continue up and over the hill ahead for around three quarters of a mile (1100 metres).

At Cliff Top House, take the tarmac lane to the right towards Crook Ness (S.P. footpath to the beach, green and yellow way-marker).

This lane becomes a tarmac footpath at the field edge (S.P. public footpath and **information board about Crook Ness on your right**).

Go down the ravine and halfway down it, go up the steps to the right (S.P. acorn sign). This is where we join the Cleveland Way. At the top of the steps, the North Sea is to your left.

The Cleveland Way was the second of twelve National Trails to open, and did so in May 1969. It is 110 miles long and takes a semi circular route from Helmsley, across the North York Moors to the sea at Saltburn, and all the way down the coast to Filey.

Follow this clear path along the cliff top, heading south.

Pass the massive farm and industrial buildings of Scalby Lodge, away to your right.

The section of coast between Scalby and Burniston has become known as the 'dinosaur coast' following recent discoveries of 18 million year old dinosaur footprints from the Jurassic era. These may be found on a raised fossilised river bed on the beach.

Continue along the cliff top path, always heading for Scarborough castle headland, visible ahead of you (S.P. Cleveland Way).

The hill mound with two masts in the distance, to the right of the castle headland, is Oliver's Mount. It is England's only natural road racing circuit for motor cycles and has been so since the first races were held in 1946. It is internationally renowned. The course is almost 2 ½ miles long and the course record attendance is almost 63,000 spectators.
Famous road racer Barry Sheene won the Gold Cup International Trophy here four times and achieved 15 race wins overall.

Continue along the clear footpath, bearing left onto Scalby Ness headland with Scalby Beck down in the valley to your right and houses on the far bank top.

Bear right at the top of the headland along the path, heading towards the castle headland and then down to the right, down two lots of cobble edged steps.

Cross Scalby Beck by the footbridge next to Old Scalby Mills Pub.

There is evidence of Roman and Viking settlement here and the village was known as Scalebi in the Domesday Book. This is an old Norse name meaning the farmstead of Scali.
The pub here was originally a 17th century watermill.

Gain the North Bay Promenade by turning to the left and with the Sea-life Aquarium on your right.

The Sea-life Centre is one of a chain of similar establishments around Europe, and the tanks contained within the unique pyramid structures house many sea creatures. It also operates as a seal, otter and turtle sanctuary.
It is open to visitors as well as having an educational function.

As you continue straight ahead round the bay, pass the beach huts to your right.
This is North Bay.
Scarborough castle is prominent on the headland ahead of you.

Scarborough's prominent and strategically important headland has been occupied by many over the centuries. It was once the site of an iron-age fort.
A bronze- age sword discovered there is on display in the castle museum.
The remains of a Roman signal station, dating from around AD370, can still be found near the cliff edge.

The current castle dates from the 1150s, and stands on the foundations of a medieval Royal fortress. The castle has seen many alterations and additions in its lifetime, and has been subjected to military action on many occasions.
It has largely been a ruin since it was the victim of long and violent sieges in the English Civil War. It was shelled and further damaged by German warships in 1914. English Heritage now own and manage this popular tourist attraction.

Follow the sea-front promenade, now called Royal Albert Drive (or on the beach, tides and weather permitting), with the North Sea to your immediate left.
The sea does not recede enough to walk all the way around the headland, so regain Royal Albert Drive where appropriate.

(Please note that at times of high tides and winds, and in certain conditions, Royal Albert Drive and Marine Drive may be closed to pedestrians and traffic. If this is the case, follow the cliff path up to your right into Scarborough town centre, to the railway station and drop left down Eastborough, to the South Bay and the Harbourside T.I.C, which is the finish line.)

Anne Bronte, of the famous literary sisters, died from consumption on 28th May 1849, in a house where the Grand Hotel now stands. There is a blue plaque at the spot.
She is buried in St. Mary's churchyard, which is just behind the castle on the headland. Anne loved the town and asked to be buried here.
She is the only member of the Bronte family not to be interred at Haworth.

Walk all the way to the headland on Royal Albert Drive, as it becomes Marine Drive at the tip of the headland.

As well as being home to several varieties of gull, the headland cliffs also have a resident pair of breeding peregrine falcons. The peregrine is the most widespread bird of prey in the world, although there are only 1400 pairs in the U.K.
These birds feed on other medium sized birds such as pigeons and small ducks.
In a swooping dive the bird reaches up to 202m.p.h. (325k.p.h), making it one of the fastest creatures on earth.
The R.S.P.B. often has a telescope situated on the Marine Drive, for the use and benefit of passers-by.

Once around the headland, still on Marine Drive, pass through the stone arch on the left, under the office of H.M. Coastguard (pictured).

Emerge into Sandside with the amusement park, Luna Park, to your left.

The lighthouse on the harbour jetty was destroyed by German bombing raids in 1914, and was not rebuilt until 1931. It now doubles as the home of Scarborough Yacht Club.

This is the harbour and South Bay.

Scarborough's South Bay is the site founded as Skaroaborg by Viking raiders, although there is evidence of stone and bronze age settlement too.
In 1252, Scarborough Fair received its Royal Charter and this event was a six week long trade festival attended by visitors from across Europe.
The Fair sadly died out in the 18th century, but is still remembered in folk song:
"Are you going to Scarborough Fair? Parsley, sage, rosemary and thyme".
In 1626, an acidic spa spring was discovered in the town and a book about the phenomenon, written in 1660, brought in floods of visitors from all over the country.
This made the town Britain's first seaside resort and it is recognised as such.
To cater for visitors in later years, the railway station in the town has the longest seat at any railway station in the world.

Walk along the footpath on the left, passing the harbour.

In 1867, the Grand Hotel opened. It can be seen ahead of you.
At the time, it was the biggest hotel in Europe and one of the biggest in the world.
It has 4 towers to represent the seasons, 12 floors to represent the months, 52 chimneys to represent the weeks, and 365 rooms for the days of the year.
It was built in a 'V' shape as a tribute to Queen Victoria.

The Harbourside T.I.C. on the South Bay marks the end of the White Rose Way.
A plaque on the outside wall marks the spot. Give it a touch! Congratulations!

At the traffic lights adjacent to Alonzi's Harbour Bar is Eastborough. To get to the town centre, simply follow this road uphill, and keep going in a straight line into the town. The railway station and bus links back to Leeds are but a short stroll away, as is the suggested bed and breakfast accommodation for those staying to enjoy the delights that Scarborough has to offer.

White Rose Way enamel pin-badges and key-rings are available, to show the world that you have walked from Leeds to Scarborough.
They are available to view and order via the 'Merchandise' page at:
www.whiteroseway.co.uk

Comments and suggestions are also welcome at:
 whiteroseway@gmail.com
These may be published on the comments page of the web-site, where appropriate.

Advertising enquiries from related businesses for inclusion on the web-site are welcome at the above e-mail address.

DISCLAIMER

Every effort has been made to ensure that this walk has clear, concise and accurate instructions. All distances given in metres are approximate.

Public Rights of Way are strictly followed in this guide but sometimes these change over time, or have temporary restrictions or diversions. Always follow the advice displayed on notices about any such changes.

If you notice any changes which materially and permanently affect this trail, please send details of the problem via e-mail to: whiteroseway@gmail.com so that it can be investigated and the trail notes amended, if necessary.

Some sections of the walk follow riverbanks and occasionally, these areas may be subject to flooding. Please take all reasonable precautions and consider alternative paths or roads where appropriate. Your safety is paramount at all times.

An on-line accommodation guide is available at www.whiteroseway.co.uk to help with the planning of the walk.
The premises detailed are merely suggestions which have been made in good faith.
A suggestion is not a recommendation.
Other accommodation is available and the choice is yours.
Any disputes arising from accommodation issues of any kind, are between the owners of the establishment concerned, and their clients.

The contact information for all of these premises is correct at the time of writing these trail notes. Changes may be notified by e-mail to; whiteroseway@gmail.com for amendment.

No responsibility can be accepted by the author or publisher of these trail notes, for any injury or claims for damages which may arise out of taking part in this trail, however they may be caused.

Happy walking.

Leeds Civic Hall

Packhorse bridge, Meanwood Park

Seven Arches Bridge, Scotland Wood

Georgian Bath House, Wetherby

JMW Turner's view, Wetherby Bridge

Bridge and weir, Wetherby

Newton Kyme Hall and church

Tadcaster bridge

Heslington Common

Lane next to Grimwith Wood

Rail and road bridges, Stamford Bridge

Bluebells at Buttercrambe

Bridge at Kirkham

Beck Isle Cottage, Thornton le Dale

Givendale Rigg

Langdale End vista

Field lane Burniston

The Dinosaur Coast, Scalby

Harbour TIC – The Finish Line!

Probably the best finish line in the World!